The Religion of
Science Fiction

The Religion of Science Fiction

Frederick A. Kreuziger

Bowling Green State University Popular Press
Bowling Green, Ohio 43403

CONTENTS

PREFACE AND ACKNOWLEDGEMENTS

No book writes itself; but neither is any critical study a singular, solitary effort. The notes appended give only one indication, however, of the fact that all criticism is a collaborative effort. Thus I must acknowledge the many different audiences to whom various portions of this book, in now I am sure unrecognizable form, were first directed. These include, in some rough semblance of order, a small study group at the University Catholic Center, Madison, graduate seminars at Marquette University, the Popular Culture Association, and the American Academy of Religion. The genuine interest, encouragement, and feedback contributed greatly to shaping the overall direction and many specifics of this study. Special thanks, finally, to the librarians at Stavanger Bibliotek and the Universitets Bibliotek in Bergen, Norway, who handled with great poise and concern the last-minute requests as this study neared completion.

Thanks will not discharge the debt to the partner, Mim. To her I dedicate the book.

Denver, Colorado   Frederick Kreuziger

INTRODUCTION

To call science fiction a religion will probably alienate as many readers as it will excite. The former, of course, is not intended; but neither is the latter. Still, it seems to be the most compelling name to give the phenomenon, what with its grandiose claims, its sweeping justifications of mankind's role in the universe, its practitioners of rituals and coteries of followers, its sects and counter-sects, saints, heretics, martyrs, bibles, and golden age—and, at length, its theologians in the form of critics.

The larger claim argued throughout this book is that science fiction functions today as a religion. Peter Berger's writings on the matter of religion from a sociological viewpoint are perhaps the most well known and accessible. In *The Sacred Canopy* he writes: "Religion implies that human order is projected into the totality of being. Put differently, religion is the audacious attempt to conceive of the entire universe as being humanly significant." This is a functional description of religion; it woiks no matter what 'humans' are being talked about, or what 'universe' is at stake. The correlation to science fiction is obvious.

The smaller focus of the book, however, is apocalyptic thought. Now, apocalypse is so loaded with doomsday imagery as to be practically inseparable from the dramas of the world's end through natural, human, or supernatural causation. Too numerous to mention are those who ride the bandwagon of apocalypse: ecologist, economist, social critic (left and right), and, in the forefront today, the anti-nuclear activists. The 'Ground Zero' scenarios are dramas of the final day: apocalypse now. To expand Berger's description we might say that apocalypse is the 'audacious attempt to conceive of the entire universe as being humanly significane *when viewed in terms of how it ends.*' Again the correlation to science fiction is obvious.

What is not so obvious, however, is that apocalypse means

1

much more than visions of the end and tales of doomsday. Its meaning cuts across the spectrum of life, both personal and social. This small book thus seeks to expand the understanding of both apocalyptic thought and science fiction. Not a small task. Let me flesh out the argument in more detail.

What is startling about apocalyptic thought and writing is that it is so much with us in our times and in our culture that we miss its obvious manifestations. In this it is helpful to speak of a secular apocalyptic in the same sense that we speak of a secular religion. The argument is not that our culture has simply borrowed from, revived, or reinterpreted apocalyptic thought in order to explain the unfolding of contemporary history (after the manner of Hal Lindsay's *The Late Great Planet Earth*, for example), but rather that our culture has become in its own way and according to its own forms apocalyptic in its outlook, its thinking, and in its image making. One can say it has reached the same point as biblical apocalyptic, but by different means.

Others have commented in far more scholarly works on the apocalyptic (millennarian, chiliastic) roots of Naziism and communism, and on the state of 'perpetual crisis' in which we seem to be living. Norman Cohn touches on the former in his *The Pursuit of the Millennium*; Frank Kermode describes the latter in his *The Sense of an Ending*. As mentioned above, any review of book titles describing the impending ecological and/or nuclear disasters will confirm the fact that apocalypse is the compelling mode of symbolization. In both we catch echoes of doomsday, Armageddon, and the final death throes of a declining, over-industrialized, self-indulgent, narcissistic civilization.

Again, this short work has a more modest aim; to read in the science fiction experience the peculiar apocalyptic transformations which inform its thinking and image-making. In this it is a commentary (albeit somewhat out of the mainstream) on the mode of popular mythology which science fiction has become, and an attempt to explore systematically the images, symbols, and themes comprising its enduring appeal. I will speak often of science fiction as a secular apocalyptic; by this I do not mean that it has no relation whatever to the biblical, religious forms. I mean simply that it has a dynamic of its own, that one need not be aware of the roots and interconnections to appreciate how its mythology, cosmology, and future history have evolved. David Ketterer's study, for example, *New Worlds for Old,* operates with the minimum of biblical grounding, and makes its case no less for that reason. But an appreciation and awareness of the roots and interconnections do help—both in understanding science fiction and in understanding biblical apocalyptic literature. Ketterer, of course, did not have the latter for his purpose. I do.

Historians, critics, fans, and commentators on the genre of science fiction have labored long and hard tracing its roots down through centuries of adventurous tales and speculative fabulation. Gilgamesh certainly deserves the honor of being the first and earliest protagonist, and Frankenstein one of the more notoriously recent. In between, the litany of forerunners includes the works of Lucian, Campanella, Bacon, de Bergerac, and Voltaire. But rarely, if ever, does one find mention of Daniel, John, Moses, Baruch, or Ezra as being among the earliest of visionaries and tellers of the future, in whose works are described planetary systems, heavenly beings, wars of the worlds, and the longed for coming of the 'new age.' In language and symbol and philosophical system, there is speculation on the future course of history (both close and distant), the meaning of current events, and the purpose of earthly existence. To the select few it has been 'revealed' the things to come; to the rest, the wisdom of that revelation remains forever hidden—or the folly of such escape is obvious. The reaction is more often than not the latter; apocalypse, biblical or secular, was and is rarely a movement of the masses, although it is always a popular literature. It is written, that is, for the people not for the critics.

Any attempt, therefore, to correct the oversight of naming apocalyptic literature as a legitimate forerunner of science fiction will have to focus on the fact that both apocalyptic and science fiction are instances of popular literature and popular culture. That is to say, the analysis will necessarily have to be as much sociological as it is literary—perhaps even more so. It will have to focus on the function of apocalyptic literature, the role it plays in the life of a society.

Thus the scope and method of this small volume. It remains only to say some few words about the plan. Chapter One presents the obvious parallels between biblical and secular apocalyptic— when viewed according to function. Even more so than borrowed imagery and symbols (of which there is much and about which much has been written) the 'borrowed' function (that of providing hope in a crisis situation) links biblical and secular apocalyptic.

Chapter Two explores the basis of this hope—the faith on which the vision of secular apocalyptic is founded. The relationship between faith and hope is critical, as the theologians of hope have made a clear. Hope is the form of faith, not the act of faith (made when everything else has failed). At the same time faith is the vision which keeps the hope alive. To understand the hope of apocalyptic, it is necessary to understand its faith.

Chapter Three returns to the hope which informs the faith. It treats of utopia, the city, the New Jerusalem, and finally doomsday, as presented in biblical and secular apocalyptic. Specifically, the issue is raised here concerning temporal or historical consciousness, as seen from the end. Life and history do not just go on and on anywhere whatever, they go somewhere.

Chapter Four explores this temporal and historical consciousness as it is dramatized in the stories of science fiction. Of particular interest is the distinction between *what* we expect in the future and *how* we expect the future to come about. The latter has obvious consequences for how we live our lives, and these will be examined.

Chapter Five takes on the case against apocalyptic. Armed with the analysis of the preceding four chapters, it is now possible to critique the arguments, theological, cultural, and literary, which dismiss apocalyptic as a corruption of prophecy, the responsible stance of the believer toward the future, showing to the contrary that apocalyptic thematizes legitimately a meaningful dimension of life.

Chapter Six, finally, presents a working synthesis, along with appropriate commentary, of the 'Future as Promise' in the many varied shapes it has taken and continues to take in theology, culture, and literature. Here the roots are traced and the final model is built.

CHAPTER ONE

THE WORD *APOCALYPSE* IN GREEK means revelation.[1] The practice of interchanging the titles of the last book of the Christian testament (Apocalypse and Revelation) bears witness to what has by now become a double meaning. Both words and both meanings, however, are contained. In the course of this book it will become more clear how they intertwine. Even further, this book will confront both those who want revelation without an end (apocalypse), and those who want an end without revelation, i.e., those who want nothing to change but themselves, and those who want everything to change but themselves.

More precisely, apocalypse means an unfolding; hence a revelation through unfolding. Here we receive the first clue as to how the content and the form of apocalypse are woven inextricably together. Focus on form (story) and focus on content (what story is about) can never really be separated. Apocalypse as story first of all reveals story as that which shapes our search for meaning. Story is the primary intent and first message of apocalyptic. Apocalyptic is the primal story. Story itself, not what it is about, gives meaning. This focus may become somewhat blurred, or even lost, in the succeeding discussions of the images and symbols of apocalyptic literature and science fiction, but it remains the central tenet of the following study.

Apocalyptic literature is an old and venerable literary genre of the Ancient Near East. The second part of the Book of Daniel, portions of Ezekiel and Isaiah in the Hebrew testament, and the Apocalypse of John in the Christian testament have subsequently been canonized by the church; that is, accepted as integral parts of the scriptures, the word of God. But there are extant in addition scores of other examples, in whole and in fragmentary form, which attest to the popularity of the form. Many were the stories told, of the future vindication of the chosen people and the fulfillment of God's promises.

The imagery found in the apocalyptic literature of the Bible is

1) Apocalyptic literature is a literature of hope, in a time of crisis. It is terrible (i.e., terrifying) consolation, but consolation nonetheless; everything will be resolved according to the plan of God.

2) The time of crisis has historical reality. But in the biblical imagination a crisis of history is always also a crisis of faith. The crisis, more precisely, is one of disillusionment, but not with the reality of the world and all its evil. It is a questioning ultimately of the "promise" of God to remain with his people.

3) The parallels to be explored in our treatment of science fiction and apocalyptic are:

A). The Apocalypse of Daniel, written to comfort those disillusioned by exile, return and the failure of the messianic kingdom to be established.
B) The Apocalypse of John, written to comfort those disillusioned by the failure of Jesus to come again (the Second Coming) and suffering now under the persecution of Rome.
C) The apocalypse of science fiction, written to comfort those disillusioned by the failure of the promise of technology and science to deliver the world from poverty, ignorance, disease, war, famine, plague, and death, and living in a world which stubbornly refuses to accept the breakthroughs made by science, relying instead on "political" answers.

To speak of a "comfort to the disillusioned" is perhaps to stress the negative side of apocalypse over the positive. The positive, of course, is that apocalyptic literature is a literature of hope. The precise comfort offered is hope, the promise that a new age is coming. But belief in and hope for the new age is also a critique of the present age, a way of saying that what now exists, the old order, is not good enough. What is being said in science fiction, therefore, is not that science and technology are evil and have irremediably failed, but rather that the order they have thus far created has failed to provide what has been promised through them. The answer to bad science, science fiction argues, is good science.

Just as the reign of God will suddenly be established, and the coming of Jesus will suddenly occur (with the consequent destruction of the old order), so too the reign of science and technology is just around the corner. It awaits only the sudden discovery of new sources of power, a cure for crippling and fatal diseases, a development of mental, psychic and telepathic powers, the invention of new modes of transportation, whatever. With these new discoveries and inventions comes the sudden eclipse of present social, economic, political and cultural structures and institutions. The end of monogamous marriage, the collapse of capitalism, the surpassing of naive religious faith—all these and more are the effects of the coming of the new heavens and the new earth, brought to us by science and technology, although not all in each case.

The obverse side of this understanding is that the age of crisis, this present time, is a period of transition. In this, as Kermode argues, it belongs neither to the past nor to the future. It is a special time, set apart and ruled, therefore, by a special ethic. We will treat of the special ethic of the technological imperative in the following chapter. But this ethic also has relevance for the understanding and use of history, both past and future. Crisis and disillusionment demand that reverence for the past and future be tempered by the needs of the present. Accordingly, new tools of interpretation are fashioned to give credence to the claim that what was said before, or what happened before, is perhaps not really what it was claimed to be. The same for the future. New tools of interpretation open up new dimensions and stories about that future. In biblical and interestamental apocalyptic, visions, dreams, and trips through the heavenly realms replace prophetic encounters with God; cosmological charts and divisions of history into specific time segments replace the story of God's special promise unfolding through historical struggle; and determinism and dualism replace the deuteronomic ethic of sin leading to misfortune and repentance leading to forgiveness. The present is what matters. Everything in apocalypse is focused on the present, no matter what the concern expressed over past history, no matter how much it speaks of turmoil leading to future glory. If the world as we know it ends tomorrow, today has special relevance and immediacy. The ethic for this period of transition is an ethic of decision—now! To put it even more simply: apocalypse is story always told in the present tense.

Apocalyptic literature is of hope in a time of crisis. It is a statement of faith and hope in the face of a world experienced as falling apart. Although the most readily remembered images and themes are those catastrophic (the great holocaust to come, doomsday, the plagues, Armageddon), apocalyptic literature is not fatalistic. It is crisis literature, concerned with what is happening at the time of the writing.

Apocalyptic literature is the product of times in which everything becomes frighteningly clear, when people realize what is at stake, when they realize it is a life and death struggle between the forces of good and evil, light and darkness, on a cosmic scale, a level which transcends the private and individual life. This life and death struggle, however, is not relegated to the end time (when that end time is seen only in the framework of evolutionary consciousness, that is, when it comes about slowly and gradually); it is always present in the life of the community, for the present, now, is the critical and important time.

The reality of the threat of evil and the promise of God to stand by and strengthen his people are valid for all times—but it is in the present where it matters most. Although the attempts by the Jehovah's Witnesses and other fundamentalist sects (and by such books as *The Late Great Planet Earth*) to interpret and apply the prophecies of Daniel and John on a one to one correspondence to modern events are misleading and ultimately futile, still they are correct in their insistence on the historical reality of the struggle.

Apocalyptic meaning is also destroyed when it is relegated to the private, individualized world of the modern self. But apocalyptic is likewise misconstrued when its primary intent is seen as "prediction." Just as history is not a mere collection of objective facts (what really happened), so future history is not the objective correspondence of events to prediction. Future history is similar to past history: the story a people tells to make sense of the unfolding of events. Just as story has a beginning, so it has an end. Apocalyptic is a literature which reveals the end—not of the world, so much, as of the story. It is not the end of the world which is demanded in apocalypse, it is the end of the story. This is the primary, objective determinism, if you will, functioning on the level of story itself.

Just what does this story mean? What is it really about? What is its purpose? Perhaps a contemporary psychologist may speak the insight to make sense of apocalyptic. In an interview in *Psychology Today* Robert Jay Lifton addresses himself to what he considers the contemporary formulation of hope which is needed, the consolation for which people hunger and thirst: a belief in the continuity of life:

I am trying to get at some of the underlying anxiety that is affecting people in every society. Our sense of the continuity of life is profoundly threatened. There is a strong undercurrent of imagery of death and technological annihilation, and it becomes increasingly difficult for people to give significant form to their ideas, their actions, and to themselves. They are no longer certain where anything begins or ends.

common, conventional and standard to much of the other literature of that genre; along with beasts, plagues and battles, there are the vision, the angel who interprets the opening of the secrets of heaven, and the messianic kingdom. The themes of apocalyptic literature are likewise conventional: the revelation of the future to come, the final period of world history, the cosmic struggle between the forces of good and evil, the fulfillment of God's promises, and the establishment of his kingdom in glory.

All these themes are explored by means of the vision which is the revelation. The vehicle for the transmission of the message is the written word. In this respect apocalyptic differs from prophecy in the strict sense, which is to be spoken by a prophet sent by God to bring judgment upon the present. The revelation of apocalypse treats of the mystery of God and human existence, the knowledge of which is not attributable to human reason. Commentators traditionally list four mysteries of which the revelation treats: 1) God and the heavenly world; 2) the origin of the world and the universe; 3) the divine plan which governs the course of history; and 4) the destiny of the individual.

To propose these areas as mysteries is already to make an act of faith; that is, to recognize that here are the important questions of life with which to wrestle. It is also to acknowledge a set of beliefs which one employs as tools in working with those mysteries, leaving aside for the present the question of whether or not the beliefs themselves are inspired. One cannot begin to understand apocalyptic literature unless one also understands (or at least recognizes the existence of) a faith which is underpinning. This is also true of science fiction.

Ever so briefly that is a description of the nature and major characteristics of apocalyptic literature. The parallels to science fiction on this level of analysis alone are already intriguing, and they present few difficulties. They are all too obvious: beasts, plagues, doomsday, Armageddon, planets and heavenly bodies, extra-terrestrial intelligences. But the parallels between apocalyptic and science fiction on the level of function and purpose are the more intriguing; and these parallels are a jumping off point for a discussion of science fiction as the contemporary "books of revelation," the modern stories which give hope to a people. What follows now is central to the argument of these brief few pages on apocalypse in science fiction. I will thus present a brief summary, then follow with a fuller treatment.

To the question whether this accounts for the apocalyptic mood seeping into everyday life, Lifton replies:

I think it does. But I also think that a certain amount of apocalyptic imagination is necessary. You find it in the more humane and searching forms of radicalism that are struggling to take shape around the world . . . . We begin with man's need, a compelling and universal urge to maintain a sense of immortality in the face of biological death. Life requires a perception of the connection extending beyond that annihilation. This need apparently has been in man's mind since his beginnings. As symbol-forming organisms we require a language to express this sense of bio-historical continuity.[2]

In the apocalypse of John, Christianity's answer to that need has not been "life after death" (or "pie in the sky," as it is commonly caricatured and dismissed—rightly, I might add), but rather "Life over death," or sometimes, "Life out of death."

Life after death would negate the meaning and purpose of Apocalypse, for it would undermine the historicity of the struggle and the value of resistance in the face of evil. It would place the resolution of that struggle outside history, thus denying the fundamental premise of all biblical faith—that God acts through history. The meaning and purpose of life is to be sought for and found in the daily struggle of mankind to bring creation (an historical datum in the biblical understanding) to fulfillment. It would be foolish to affirm the canonicity of the Apocalypse of John, and then at the same time affirm that it contradicts the consensus theology of the remainder of the Bible.

Life over death, goodness over evil, light over darkness, the lamb over the beast—all these situate the meaning and purpose and fulfillment of life in the world and in its history. This is not to say, however, that the meaning and purpose of this life is to be found in this world on the primary sensory level, but rather in the struggle to bring this world to its final consummation. The affirmation of life over death affords us the tool, as Lifton would say we need, to determine where things begin and end, to give form and shape to the struggles we engage in, to say in the end that all is worth while because we have this belief and vision against which to measure it, and primarily because we have this promise.

In the biblical understanding it is the function of apocalyptic literature to affirm the validity of the promise in a time of crisis. The specific biblical world view, however, is always one of God's promise, rarely of humankind's meaning, purpose, or fulfillment. It is not until recently that the transference has been made to speaking of the latter (as Lifton does). This has come about due to the influence of phenomenology, sociology and psychology. The story in the Bible is always a story about God in the first place; in the second place it is about what happens to humankind because of God's actions.

When one looks at the crises to which apocalyptic literature addresses itself, one discovers the complexities of those crises and the different levels on which they operate: political struggle, economic game plan, military strategy, nationalistic ambition, theological squabbling and personal vendetta. Truly there is nothing new under the sun. But it would be a great mistake to concentrate only on that level. The one new thing introduced in biblical thought is that a crisis of history is always also a crisis of faith. To be more specific, the particular dimension of the crisis which gives rise to the creation of apocalyptic literature is that of a profound disillusionment. The disillusionment, moreover, centers not on the world but on the promise of God. It is not so much the world which has failed as it is the promise of God which has dimmed, flickered and for some expired.

Apocalytic literature actually premises itself on the very opposite analysis of how a people will react to adversity than the one to which we have become accustomed. The threat of some external force or power, and the imminent collapse of "Law and Order" do not inevitably unite a people on the deepest level of their lives, their identity and their meaning. In the end, such threats often divide a people from their dreams, sever them from their hopes, and cut them off from what is most real to them: the struggle to live together.

There is an obvious example of this in our own recent times (an example, frighteningly enough, which seems to be coming around again on the merry-go-round of history): The threat of communist aggression through nuclear attack temporarily and superficially united Americans in the late Forties, through the Fifties and even into the Sixties. Because they recall a solution as well as the problem, the McCarthy hearings are the most often cited example of the crisis. But recalling those hearings alone is quite selective, and only reinforces the view that we can see our way through a false unity, or that "the system works." The more quickly forgotten, and therefore the more deeply revealing response to the "Red Menace" must also be recalled. Civil defense, Conelrad, and bomb shelters became the watchwords for national unity in the face of external threat. The fear within drove all sorts of wedges between people; the most obvious symbolic manifestation being the exclusivity of the bomb shelters. This will be taken up shortly.

Here there is a parallel to be drawn between bomb shelters and privatized eschatology—the kind which speaks of "life after death" as the goal of life. Both are concerned with "saving one's soul" almost exclusively. The major aim of both is to assure a blessed afterlife—either in heaven or on earth. The price one pays in the "bomb shelter" ethic is obvious—hoarding, mistrust, paranoia, preoccupation with self—but it may also be in order to assess the privatized eschatology ethic the same costs. At any rate, it is a high price, the hidden cost of which is revealed only much later.

Apocalyptic is a communal literature, a public and political statement about the crisis which threatens a people's identity. A word of caution is in order here. Apocalyptic is not political in the sense that it is a plan for action. It is rather a story which interprets. Apocalyptic functions as the horizon of history, as the end to (of) the story. To "implement" apocalypse results only in the chiliastic excesses of the 15th and 16th centuries in Northern Europe, as chronicled in Norman Cohn's book.[3] To implement apocalypse as plan of action in our day results in the terrorists' blind attempts to destroy the old so that the new may come. This is not what "life over death" means: life over death is the promise, not the plan.

It is the profound interior disillusionment to which apocalyptic literature addresses itself, the disillusionment which rises out of the crisis, resulting from the apparent failure of the promise, or the failure of the apparent promise (which we will take up shortly). It is this interior disillusionment to which the Apocalypse of John addresses itself; and it does so in the best tradition of apocalyptic literature. Certainly there was a crisis affecting the early church. The persecutions waged by Nero and Domitian were decimating the small band of believers. It would be misleading, however, to premise the composition of John's Apocalypse merely on the grounds that all the author was trying to say was that this particular external threat would pass and the church would survive—as though, that is, persecution alone were the crisis. Or to say it did not matter what happened in this world, because God would triumph in the next. Apocalyptic is neither the literature of escape (the next world is all that matters); nor is it the literature of revolution (this world is all that matters). It is the literature of hope.

The Apocalypse of John was concerned with a far more profound threat facing the church, an internal threat which struck to the heart of the faith. The particular historical crisis which raised this threat was not really the persecutions (the apparent failure of the promise, insofar as God did not intervene), but rather the realization that the Second Coming had to be re-thought in light of what was happening (the failure of the apparent promise, insofar as Jesus did not return in physical glory). The disillusionment arising out of consideration of the second issue struck to the very heart of the biblical faith, because it raised the one real question the Apocalypse of John had to answer and resolve: Did God act within history or outside it? In this life, or only in the next? Was it life after death or life over death?

Again it must be stated succinctly: the Apocalypse of John argues for life over death. It places the resolution of the struggle inside this world and inside history. It reaffirms the continuity and oneness of life and history. It situates the meaning and purpose and fulfillment of life in this world and its history, stretching all the way from the creation of the world to the coming of the new heavens and the new earth. It affords us the tools with which to determine where things begin and where they end, to give form and shape to the struggles in which we engage, to say that all is worthwhile because we have this belief, this vision, and this promise against which to measure it.

There remains, however, one final dimension of this topic to explore. It concerns the manner of responding to the disillusionment which inhabits the land.

There is dark optimism pervading the Apocalypse of John. Things always get worse before they get better. Plagues and pestilence erupt like roman candle fireworks across the sky; each projectile spews out further horrors. The seventh plague invariably unleashes seven more, and so on down through the seemingly masochistic imagination of the author. In the face of all this, the Apocalypse of John invites courage, hope, responsibility, awe and a holding fast to the faith. There is no invitation to escape the crisis of the times by fleeing the world, either physically or mentally (physical or philosophical suicide). Neither is there an invitation to embrace the life after death caricature of apocalyptic, for that is merely an escape into the future. John himself writes from a prison island where he is being detained for having preached the good news. Nor is there an invitation to despair or apostasy. Finally, there is no invitation to revolution, to overthrow the oppressive government, for that is merely an escape into the present. There will arise only another beast, and another, and a dragon and an anti-Christ, and so on till the final consummation of the world.

What is the invitation then? It is this: to wrestle with the beast of despair and the dragon of disillusionment who inhabit the soul of the community of believers. Things always get worse before they get better. There is good cause to fear the future, says the Apocalypse of John, even more so than the present. But that is not all; for in one swift and frightful opening of insight, when all of time is laid out before us, spread out in those few chapters (much the same way in which time travel and time machines will do it in science fiction), the realization hits home: There is good cause to fear the present even more so than we thought for the only future which counts in the end is the one which breaks suddenly into the present.

Now is waged the ultimate battle of good against evil, life against death, light against darkness. And the battle wages on, to be decided by the choices we make, for the battleground is discovered to be our conscience. The ultimate mask of reality is stripped away.

Science fiction and apocalypse are mutually illuminating. This in itself is not a startling thesis. But the interest heightens when it is noted that both science fiction and apocalyptic are considered to be marginal; that is, they exist on the margin of respectable fields of study: literature and theology. They can also be considered marginal because they are read by people who live on the margin of society. Again, it is not merely the language, characters, symbols or images which invite comparison between apocalyptic and science fiction. Or better, the comparison between the two should not stop at this level. What is needed now is to trace the structural and functional similarities between them. This will support the claim that science fiction functions as a secular apocalyptic literature.

What do people believe about the energy crisis, for example? Or any other major questions of twentieth century life in these United States? The answers inevitably reflect the scientific/technological bent of our thinking. What is needed? New energy sources, a pollution-free source of transportation, a cure for cancer, genetic engineering, and so forth. The stories people tell about themselves include a solution to the pressing problems of the age. The thesis can thus be advanced: The secular apocalyptic literature of science fiction comforts and gives hope to those who are disillusioned by the failure of science and technology to deliver the world from ignorance, poverty, disease, famine, plague, war and death.

Even as the world is destroyed a thousand times, so there remains a remnant to carry on, to persevere, to preserve the arts and the sciences, and to rebuild the earth. Even as the world dies in the throes of pollution, over-population and the ravaging of its resources, so new worlds of different suns and different galaxies are opened up to become the home for the homeless, the new promised land. Even as tyrants and demagogues and dictators enslave the human race through genetic engineering and mind control, through drugs and behavior modification, so people are liberated by the excalibur of technology, wielded by Arthurian giants. Philip Jose Farmer's book *Doc Savage: His Apocalyptic Life* chronicles this dimension of science fiction and its savior role.[4]

There is one basic assumption underlying all this: science fiction is written for "believers." Its language, its fantasy, its laws of time and space, of robots and aliens, and its conventions of time travel, hyper space, parsecs, alternate worlds and telepathy, are for the initiated, for those believers who have made the leap of faith (or not made the leap of un-faith). Belief in this context simply means being technological creatures caught up in the scientific world view. In this respect alone science fiction is remarkably akin to apocalyptic literature with its language, fantasy, laws and conventions—all indications of the fact that biblical apocalyptic, too, is for the initiated. For this reason we can, without exaggeration, refer to the Apocalypse of John as the science fiction of the Bible.

But there is a further assumption to be made. The nature of science and technology can and ought to be understood in religious terms. This will be treated at length in the subsequent chapters. Therein it will be argued that there is a mythology and ritual underlying science and technology, a set of beliefs, a sacred language, and finally a code of ethics. In all this I am not arguing that science fiction has the same meaning, the same message, the same content as the Apocalypse of John, for example. I am only contending that its role, its function today, given the assumption of the religious nature of science and technology as portrayed in science fiction literature, is similar. Namely it is to comfort and give hope to those who are disillusioned by the failure of science and technology to deliver the world from its miseries.

For better or worse the spirit of science and technology inhabits the land; it has breathed new life into contemporary humankind. In a sense it has created the modern human race. McLuhan has oracled the emergence of the electronic person; Buckminster Fuller has penned the apologia for technology; and Jacques Ellul has witnessed to the demons residing therein. Science fiction, in its own way, has also produced a chronicle; but it has done so through the literary form of the short story and the romance. In this body of writing it has created a story which scientific and technological humankind wants to hear—secular apocalypse, the final revelation of the triumph of its promise.

Science fiction, however, is not the only manifestation of secular apocalyptic in our times, just one which presents more possibilities of comparative analysis than any other. It may be helpful to catalogue some of the others, before tackling head-on the faith informing science fiction, in other words to make clear how any apocalyptic functions. In addition, the themes of crisis, hope and the sudden, radical breaking of the future into the present will be seen over and over again.

In popular culture of recent—I mean looking back some ten or fifteen years—apocalyptic has surfaced in some revealingly undisplaced forms, just enough to invite a closer look. The examples which follow are illustrative, not exhaustive. They may document a pattern, but they do not prove a thesis. They merely suggest that apocalyptic is alive and well, and that it has a peculiar function to play: to provide hope. Some of the examples border on science fiction, some do not. To be honest, the examples are those noticed as I sifted through memories of days gone by. Others I am sure will reach into their own grabbag of remembrances and come up with a different handful. So be it. Just as I read science fiction before ever having been taught how to read it, so I read apocalypse—or it was read to me—in various forms of popular culture without the guidance of scholarly thought. Here were all these images floating around in the daily rhetoric, music, and analysis of those crisis years. Readers of science fiction never forget the first book to turn them on: I'll never forget my first acquaintance with apocalyptic. It was neither mysterious, secret nor inscrutably symbolic at all—it was "right on!" I may not have agreed with all that it said, but I knew what was being said.

It begins, after all this preliminary talk, with the October 31, 1970 issue of the *Black Panther Party Newspaper*. It was the Halloween issue, to be sure. On the cover, beneath the headline, "Trick or Treat, Pigs, Trick or Treat," lies a giant orange pumpkin, its lid ready to be blown off by sticks of dynamite lodged in the opening. The fuse is already sparkling. The face of the pumpkin is sad, the corners of the mouth hang limp, tears flow, running down its cheeks. Through its eyes peer the apotheosis of the American electoral system, the end result of what was (is) offered to the American people: A Nixon and an Agnew. A heavily armed, gas-masked policeman stares at the reader through its cut-out nose. Across the lid of the pumpkin is written the legend "BABYLON."

One has only to read for a short while in the Apocalypse of John to realize that the references to Babylon are really references to Rome, the immediately experienced repressive government of the era of that book. The transference of the name Babylon to the government in Washington is easily made. A comparison of the language and the rhetoric also reveals the influence of apocalyptic imagery. We read inside the issue: "To the pigs of the power structure we are saying these are your final hours, because Babylon is falling, and upon the blood and bones of the racist revolutionary pig cops will be founded a new society." But the Apocalypse of John is not to be outdone: "He cried out in a loud voice: 'She has fallen! The great Babylon has fallen. She is now haunted by demons and unclean spirits; all kinds of filthy and hateful birds live in her. For she gave her wine to the peoples and made them drink it—the strong wine of her immoral lust. The kings of the earth committed immorality with her and the businessmen of the world grew rich from her unrestrained lust' " (Rev. 18:2-3).

The language of the Black Panthers was undisplaced apocalyptic imagery and rhetoric. The transference of images and names and symbols was made on an almost one to one basis: Washington was substituted for Rome, Nixon for Nero, pigs for beasts, and, not to be forgotten, a new society for a new heaven and a new earth.

There were numerous other examples of undisplaced apocalyptic rhetoric and imagery which exploited the feelings of those times, when the Vietnam war and the draft were "persecuting the believers." Jerry Rubin included it in his book, *Do It!* William Stringfellow essayed the faults of "Babylon" in book after article after speech. The "Liberated Church," born of radical movements, chanted the choruses of the Apocalypse of John in its liturgies. All of this was rather standard and traditional in its application, insofar as its imagery was very much tied to present conditions of society, and even more precisely as it symbolized the manifestations of the beast, the whore, in the person or the personalization of the government in Washington. There were few cosmic, speculative dimensions to this particular use of apocalyptic imagery.

Apocalyptic is a political and a politicizing literature. Its function is to name, analyze and condemn the corrupting presence of government, to pass judgment on the repressive, depersonalizing structures of power. It unites a community of believers in the common use of symbols and imagery to tell their story. To be sure, there is always present the danger of a somewhat morbid satisfaction at the passing away of the old order; always a desire to see things get worse. Critics will say this is so because it vindicates the "vision" of the believers; they are proved right. The old order was indeed corrupt! Much the same criticism is often made of the readers and writers of dystopian and post-catastrophe science fiction. As will be evident, reflecting on what was said above about the dark optimism of apocalypse, what we have here is nothing other than a realization that all reality in the end is provisional. What endures is the sense that the passage will be smoothly completed without any disturbance. There are terrible events coming, which will try the faith and hope of all believers. Best always to remember that, lest in the end one mourns the passing of the old instead of welcoming the new.

Apocalypse ultimately invites personal decision—but always in the context of community, always in terms of rejecting politically repressive powers and opting for the company of the elect. Apocalypse is not "taking Jesus for one's personal savior," and then continuing on with life as usual in the marketplaces and social arenas of the world. Nor is it some transcendental head-trip through the neural circuits of the body, a practice in levitation during the world's crumbling into chaos. There is a way of personalizing apocalypse without privatizing and individualizing it; in this form the life over death struggle becomes a community concern and a political issue.

Let Bob Dylan be the spokesperson for this dimension of apocalypse as it appears in popular song. Dylan lifts the use of apocalyptic imagery out of excessive concern with ideological matters (the saved *versus* the pigs) and political tactics (how to overthrow the beast/whore). In Dylan, apocalyptic embraces not only the meaning of the present condition, but the future transformations as well. It is impossible to place too great an emphasis on this point: the early Bob Dylan is apocalyptic to the core. It is this dimension which gives a unity and an enduring strength to his early works.

It begins with his second album, *The Free Wheelin' Bob Dylan*. The title is characteristic of Dylan's style and the style of the times, the loose, high-flying style which feeds on coincidence as the primary relationship. It is this style which illuminates the content of his songs; for his style is an appropriate response to the wedding which has taken place between apocalypse and the nuclear holocaust in the minds of the people. Dylan sings his way through America's hidden and repressed fears of the Bomb, confronting the fantasies and nightmare visions people had either blocked from their waking minds or "gutsed" their way through with the bravado and stone-walling which only Americans can manage. Dylan warms up to the topic in "I Shall be Free," a talking blues commentary on the faults and foibles of the American dream. It is almost in the spirit of good, clean fun that he picks apart the inconsistencies, the sham and the facade. His first reference to the Bomb is made cautiously:

> Late one day in the middle of the week
> eyes were closed, I was half asleep
> I chased me a woman up a hill
> right in the middle of an air-raid drill.[5]

Only half asleep (that is, only half awake) he managed to see what was happening because of the bomb shelter syndrome: all kinds of "things" were getting in the way. " Talkin' World War III Blues" presents the whole picture. A doctor thinks the singer is crazy when he says that "a world war passed through my brain," and is invited to talk about it. The telling about it again chronicles the crumbling world of America, all its gadgets and conveniences strangely out of joint. Two verses deserve further mention. Wandering around in a devastated New York City, Dylan sings: "I rung me a fall-out shelter bell. 'Give me a string bean, I'm a hungry man.' A shotgun fired and away I ran." The detail of the fall-out shelter bell explodes the scene wide open. Later he finds a girl and says: " 'Let's go play Adam and Eve.' My heart was thumping. She said, 'Hey, man, you crazy or something. You seen what happened the last time they started'." Dylan strikes at the catastrophe, the slow death which is being caused, not prevented, by the fall-out shelters. Surely it is a "bad dream."[6]

From this album on, however, Dylan does not address himself directly to the matter of air raids, fall-out shelters, bombs or holocausts. Yet the imagery and intent becomes more frightening and more clear. Particularly in "A Hard Rain's A-Gonna Fall," Dylan comes close to stripping away the masks of ultimate reality. There is everything at stake now, in the impending holocaust. Meaning and reality much more profound than national security and honor, than free world *versus* communist, than survival of the American way of life is at stake. Dylan travels through the "guts" of life in this song; all reality cries out to be touched, tasted, listened to. Nature has finally revolted; people are lost and desperate, for everything has been turned around. (One is reminded here both of the "nausea" of Jean Paul Sartre, and the statement of Romano Guardini: "To understand the Apocalypse one must first of all free oneself from the conception of things' rigidity."[7]) Dylan himself reveals his own desperation when he says of the song: "It is a desperate kind of song. Every line in it actually is the start of a whole song. But when I wrote it, I thought I wouldn't have enough time alive to write all those songs. So I put all I could into this one."[8] It was written during the Cuban missle crisis of October 1962.

What Dylan does in his songs is lift the use of apocalyptic imagery out of the very narrow confines of political ideology, and bring it to bear on the transcendent forces of good and evil shaping people's lives. What matters is not so much doomsday itself, but the fear of, or the transformation by means of doomsday. The theater of Dylan is thus broadened to include all of life. No longer is the government seen to be the primary cause of the chaos which exists, nor the primary target of Dylan's barbs. The "hard rain" falls on everyone's parade.

The second side of *Bringing It All Back Home* presents another facet of Dylan's style and commentary. Dylan's vehicle here is the dream, a vision helped along by drugs. His style is to poke fun at and hold up the mirror to humankind. The troubadour, the wandering minstrel, the court jester—he is all these and more. He is the mystic who sees all and tells all. He is the tambourine man. But the songs on side two are a personal tale, too; for they are an effort to work through the question whether it is worthwhile continuing as troubadour, standing up there in front of everyone. The drugs of "Tambourine Man" bring visions, strip the senses, lead everywhere in the "jingle, jangle morning"—all the way from the Garden of Eden to Ma (Mom, Mother) and the breaking of all former ties. In the end he sings "It's all over now, Baby Blue." But it is not the cosmic holocaust of which he now sings; it is the personal transformation: one should leave everything behind and "strike another match, go start anew."[9]

In the end, then, Dylan makes it through on a slightly different level of imagery: "It's all over now, Baby Blue" signals a shift in meaning. Apocalypse for Dylan has become personal apocalypse; it leads to *Highway 61 Revisited* and the song about "Desolation Row." The mask is completely stripped away and the vision is one of hell. We will see later how this is a necessary step in the creative workings of the apocalyptic imagination. But it is precisely Dylan's failure to contend with the very real and formidable technological forces causing the fear, the desperation, and the loneliness which result in his subsequent searching being an exploration only of his private, individual self. Apocalypse reduced to this level leads only to sentimental views of life, love, happiness—views which Dylan caricatured so deftly in his early days.

Dylan's musical career parallels the inevitable dead-end nature of excessive concern with individual self-fulfillment. Vapid, sweet, maudlin and insipid are all rather weak adjectives to use in describing Dylan and his music between *Highway 61 Revisited* and *Blood on the Tracks*. Some earlier critics have decried Dylan's turn to the electronic medium (first employed in *Bringing It All Back Home*) as the beginning of the end. But perhaps that was just the nature of the beast. Amplified sound merely magnifies the lack of content, wherever it occurs. Certainly one cannot fault "Idiot Wind" or "Hurricane" of *Blood on the Tracks*, nor the entire *Hard Rain* album for lacking the critical force of his early albums. *Hard Rain* is a case in point; it is "Dylan Revisited." What Dylan does in this album is re-interpret many of his earlier songs (but including also a few from his wasted years), casting them now in the spirit of desperation which underlay the "hard rain" plea in its initial appearance. It is one thing to look inside and see the hard rain of someone else's twisted vision destroying all that one holds dear; it is quite another to look inside and see oneself as part of the problem. "Lay, Lady, Lay" of *Nashville Skyline*, a ballad to the intoxicating aura of sensual delight, becomes in *Hard Rain* an expose of the technological dilemma of "having your cake and eating it too." In the mechanical fulfillment of all desire comes the end of desire.

Perhaps it is fitting to conclude our survey of Dylan on the note of desire. It is the title of his next album. A major characteristic of apocalyptic is that it induces desire; for hope is grounded much more in desireability than in possibility. This is also the message of science fiction. Of the myriad possibilities which science and technology hold up before a mesmerized humankind, science fiction singles out and portrays the desireable (or the undesireable, as the case may be, in dystopian science fiction). Expectation, rather than extrapolation, is the form of science fiction, dictating its dreams and visions of things to come.[10] In Dylan's case one can only wonder whether the real desire has now expressed itself, the "reborn" Dylan of *Slow Train Coming*. Even here, however, we encounter Dylan Revisited. For the apocalyptic vision is repeated, now in overtly biblical terms. The "hard rain" has washed him clean.

But let us turn one final time to the world of popular music, to explore further this relationship between the possible and the desireable, particularly as it is presented to us in the technological imperative: What can be done, must be done.

Jefferson Airplane provides us our final look at the resurgence of apocalyptic in popular music, as well as an example of how apocalyptic is a message of hope. The music of Jefferson Airplane also begins with social/political commentary, moves to the doomsday theme, and ends finally in the transformation of humankind. In the course of this passage, the group itself evolves from Jefferson Airplane to Jefferson Starship.

Unlike Dylan, Jefferson Airplane follows through on the apocalyptic imagery; their deliverance is expected and accomplished (in song at least) in the same terms as their disillusionment. The other edge of the two-edged sword of technology is honed for the coming battle. Technology is reconciled with the world of the radicals and revolutionaries; the possible becomes the content of the desireable.

Crown of Creation is the doomsday world of Jefferson Airplane. The album cover itself is a parable of the present crisis. One must picture it: "Crown of Creation" written in flaming letters at the base of the golden-orange mushroom cloud. Nuclear warfare spells the dead end for humankind. It is both the ultimate weapon and the ultimate form of pollution. Superimposed on the mushroom cloud, moreover, are the pictures of people. That the people are the Jefferson Airplane is itself significant; for it proclaims the end of their innocence. The lesson is brought home in all its horror: as creator of the ultimate weapon and form of pollution, humankind is both the victim and the executioner. The bomb is mirror to the fact that all life is woven together so inextricably that to unravel any part of it in the end tears the whole fabric apart.

The songs of the album detail the doomsday world already created by the very presence of the bomb. This is witness to the fact that to have built the bomb is already to have pushed the button. Dylan made the same point in his songs about fall-out shelters. Jacques Ellul argues in *The Technological Society* that the whole dynamics of technology is irreversible. Once the first step is made, for example, once the atom was split and its destructive force became known, there was no choice but to build the bomb. The bomb is symbol of where technological society is taking us according to the logic of the technological imperative. But there are other "first steps" according to Jefferson Airplane: electronic data banks reduce us all to faceless ciphers, waiting in endless lines; and freeway's "concrete ways" lead us more quickly than ever to the end. "Star Track" (a reference to "Star Trek"?) contains the plea:

> You can fool your friends
> about the way it ends,
> but you can't fool yourself.[11]

And in a delightfully mixed-metaphor title, "Ice Cream Phoenix" the question is raised:

> Tell me why if you think you know
> Why people love when there's no tomorrow
> And still not cry when it's time to go.[12]

Phoenix, a mythical bird which rises from the ashes, has long been a favorite name for spaceships in science fiction. But even the hope for tomorrow melts away, like ice cream, in the ashes of nuclear war.

The title song, "Crown of Creation," is an allusion to the ambiguous situation of the human race. At first glance, it may appear to celebrate the message of the psalmist, who sings in Psalm 8: "When I behold the heavens, the works of your hands, the moon and stars which you set in place, what is man that you should be mindful of him, or the son of man that you should care for him? You have made him a little less than the angels, and crowned him with honor and glory." As a matter of fact, the lyrics are taken almost verbatim from *Re-Birth*, a post-holocaust science fiction novel by John

Wyndham. The new world after the holocaust is one of mutation; examples abound everywhere, animal, vegetable, human. A settlement of true believers dedicates itself to the proposition, or in religious terms accepts the dogma, that all mutants are evil; God did not intend such for creation. Mutants are systematically and ritually rooted out; even the mutant sons and daughters are sent off to the "hinterlands." The one mutation which is not visibly apparent, however, is telepathy. The plot centers on the plight of the children born with that power. They are gradually discovered; they escape only because one of them, with enormous telepathic powers, is able to contact another settlement half way around the world, and a ship is sent to rescue them. The rescuer is the person who speaks the lyrics of the song: "You are the crown of creation / and you've got no place to go—"[13]

The lyrics are chosen from a passage which argues that humankind has worked itself into a deadend by refusing to change, adapt and grow.[14]

The final song of the album, "House at Pooneil Corners," also describes the loss of innocence: war cannot be stopped by tears. There is an obvious allusion in the title to the adventures of Winnie the Pooh and the story "The House at Pooh Corners." The world, our home, has been stolen, spirited away from us in the middle of the night, and refashioned into a "better" world. We are no longer at home, however, in a world transformed by technology: we are homeless, "All the idiots have left."[15]

The obvious solution to the analysis undertaken in *Crown of Creation* is given in a further album by the Jefferson Airplane, now transformed into Jefferson Starship. The album, *Blows Against the Empire*; and the solution: "Highjack the starship; / carry 7000 people past the sun."[16] They argue further: "Genesis is not the answer to what there was before." They mean by this not only that nostalgia is a bum trip, but also that innocence is no longer a viable option. In the secular religion, when paradise is lost, it can no longer be regained. But it can be created through the choices we make. This is the critical turn taken by Jefferson Starship. The choices taken from this time on have to do with science and technology. Specifically, what Jefferson Starship argues for is a reassessment of our stance toward technology. *Crown of Creation* was the clincher in the death of a naive optimism that technology is the salvation of humankind. The building of the bomb is the "original sin" of the inhabitants of the garden of technology. The destruction of the house at Pooneil corners is the most recent version of the myth of the homeless condition of humankind after their expulsion from that garden. Highjacking the starship is the story of Moses leading the people from slavery into the promised land. But it is also the parable of people caught in the human condition, never really knowing good from evil, but nevertheless having one's actions participate in both. People must still, however, choose. And the choice urged is to be responsible to themselves and to the future, to use science and technology in the exercise of that responsibility. The past is not the answer to what there was before; only the future is. This is not escape, it is "letting go." "You gotta let go, you know, or else you stay." Here is another allusion to the exodus story. It is the illusion that all technology is destructive and must be relinquished. In the end it is technology which is the occasion for the final transformation of humankind:

> At first I was irridescent
> Then I became transparent
> Finally I was absent.[17]

Humankind goes the way of God, it seems.

By way of concluding footnote, lest there be any hesitation in making the obvious link between "Starship" and the messages of science fiction, Jefferson Starship does so itself. In the list of acknowledgements contained in the album liner, one reads the legend: "Thanks to Kurt Vonnegut, Robert Heinlein, Buckminster Fuller, Theodore Sturgeon." One can only wonder why they did not also list John Wyndham.

The resurgence of apocalyptic imagery coincides with the resurgence of science fiction. Why is this so? Perhaps because both apocalyptic and science fiction require a "letting go" of the illusions of reality, a denial of "things' rigidity." And the greatest illusion, the most rigid of mental restraints is that the possible alone dictates the future. Both apocalyptic and science fiction present us with the dimension of desire. Further: It is the form of this desire (much more so than the content) which links apocalyptic with science fiction. For the form of this desire is story. Both apocalyptic and science fiction tell a story about the future of things to come. What people desire above all is a story which makes sense of what lies ahead, and nonsense of what is happening now. Thus the dark optimism' of apocalyptic; for it must needs destroy the existing order of things and disclaim as false the story now being told about the present.

The popularity of *Star Trek* can be traced to this function, that it tells a story which makes sense of the future and nonsense of the present. The frequent allusions to the backwardness and moral infancy of pre-Federation humankind is the necessary other side of the coin which tells the future glory of humankind. Much the same can be said for *Star Wars, Close Encounters of the Third Kind, 2001: A Space Odyssey, Soylent Green, Silent Running, A Boy and His Dog, Rollerball,* and even *Battlestar Galactica.* They and the host of other current science fiction stories, on film or in book, are part of the story humankind desires to hear; for they make a sense of an uncertain future. In this they are all, to some degree, apocalyptic.

CHAPTER TWO

IN THE DAYS IMMEDIATELY FOLLOWING the Three Mile Island nuclear power plant alert, many a commentator remarked on the tendency real life has of following fiction. The coincidental release of *The China Syndrome*, a major motion picture depicting a similar crisis, was featured in almost every news story and television report. In addition, Walter Cronkite, introducing an hour long *CBS Reports*, chronicled humankind's long history of courting disaster by meddling with the forces of nature. He cited Prometheus stealing fire from the gods and Frankenstein creating the monster, as stories which told of the stormy courtship and its dangers.

The underlying message of such commentary is that fiction (in our case, science fiction) is realistic and predictive in nature. Much of it is; but to relegate science fiction to the role of "predicting" and foretelling is to miss the many other functions it serves. Similar uses have been made of apocalyptic literature, wherein "kingdoms" have been juggled to coincide with certain secular reigns, the weeks and days mentioned in various writings have been calculated to foretell the establishment of the messianic age, and the signs and portents read to predict the final battle of Armageddon.

What is missing in the above commentary and reading of science fiction and apocalypse is an awareness that, when speaking of the future, life *must* imitate fiction. This should cause neither surprise nor wonder. For life, insofar as it is historical, insofar as it is unfolding of events, is a fiction. When asked who we are, for example, we give a name first, then we tell a story—personal, cultural, racial, national. Indeed our names are themselves summaries of larger stories, as was evidenced by *Roots*. And the "fiction" of the television presentation *Holocaust* was much more powerful and stirring than ever were the "facts" of Buchenwald, Auschwitz and Dachau.

The use, then, of the fact of a nuclear power plant alert to prove the validity and relevance of fiction and science fiction, or the similar use of some natural disaster to underscore the realism of *Earthquake*, *The Towering Inferno*, or even *Jaws*, is to put the cart before the horse, or in science fiction time travel jargon the son before the father who invents the time machine to become his own father. Fiction, or story, mediates life; it does not predict or foretell the events of life. In simpler terms, story interprets, story does not plan, explain or control. The relevance of Prometheus and Frankenstein is not that they predicted or foretold what would happen if humankind interfered with the natural order of things; it is that they provided the tools with which to understand and make sense of events happening at the time they were written. The surprise, then, is not in the prediction, but in the fact that humankind continues .to create situations in which the stories are still relevant.

The stories of Prometheus and Frankenstein have achieved the status of myth in this regard; for myth is nothing more than a communal story told to help a people make sense of their lives. It provides order in the midst of chaos, meaning in the face of absurdity. When story does achieve the status of myth then life must imitate·it: for the the primary drive of humankind is toward meaning and order, toward making sense of the overwhelming complexity of facts and data bombarding us.

More and more, the "story" of science fiction is achieving such a status. More and more, people are talking of the search for extraterrestrial intelligent life, the exploration of the solar system, the increasing longevity of life, the breakthrough to new systems of energy, and so on—and more often than not in terms and symbols and images long used in the stories of science fiction. Slowly, then, the names in science fiction stories are given to real life projects: the "Enterprise" space shuttle is but one example.

Myth has always been a common ground for the study of the relationship between religion and literature. And so it is in this analysis. The movement of myth has usually been studied as originating in religion (the primitive drive) and culminating in literature. Thus the Epic of Gilgamesh, the first three chapters of the Book of Genesis, the Epic of Beowulf, and the Iliad and the Odyssey of Homer. But there is no reason that the order cannot be reversed, no reason that the stories of a people cannot become their religion. This is the argument of Northrop Frye in his small volume *The Secular Scripture*. The intent of this present chapter is similar: to explore the stories of science and technology which have become the modern myths, the secular scripture, and which have culminated in a secular religion. This is another facet of our claim that science fiction is secular apocalyptic literature. The following analysis tries to go beyond the simple designation of science and technology as a deity, in order to speak of the "salvation" which it promises. For it is a promise which lies at the heart of apocalypse.

Before we are aware of most anything in this life, we are aware that science and technology save. This awareness is so close to our being that it can be said to constitute us as modern humankind. To speak of the soteriological aspect of science and techology shocks us for two reasons: 1) it exposes a faith-dimension in our lives which is by and large pre-conscious; and 2) it reminds us that no matter how sophisticated are our technological achievements and scientific breakthroughs, we are, for all that, still one with (so-called) primitive humankind in our concern about salvation. Any systematic study, therefore, of the mythic-religious nature of science and technology will have to come to grips with its pre-conscious faith dimension, with the pre-understanding which grounds its world view. This pre-understanding is what many theologians often refer to as an "existential faith implicit in our existence," that is, the basic confidence humankind has in its environment. It is the purpose of this chapter to explore this pre-understanding.

Rather than remain on this abstract, theoretical level, however, let us move to a concrete example of how the story we tell about science and technology saves us from the chaos of meaninglessness. The following advertisement appeared in a local midwestern newspaper shortly after the Arab oil embargo, when the American way of life—as based on present day energy technologies—was being seriously questioned. Written for an automobile dealership by its president, it extends far beyond selling cars to give expression to a faith view which undergirds all of life. I will cite the argument in its entirety, but add appropriate commentary throughout.

WONDERFUL AUTO WORLD
TELLING THE STORY OF BUSINESS

The horizon is definitely mythic; a world is going to be talked about, in terms of a story. We are therefore grounded in a familiar cosmos, the world of the auto. This cosmos is fashioned through the telling of a story; it is friendly, it gives security, it gives meaning. In this world we are safe from the terror of chaos.

IT'S TIME TO OPEN OUR EYES AND LOOK WITH UNDERSTANDING

Besides reminding us of Jesus' injunction that we open our eyes and see, our ears and hear, we are also reminded of Paul's refrain: "Now is the time of salvation!" In more current theological talk, we are reminded of Bultmann's statement that the kerygma calls for an existential response of faith here and now.

FOR THOUSANDS OF YEARS WE HAVE FOLLOWED THOSE WHO HAVE SAID: "YOU'RE YEARS AHEAD OF OUR TIME." "WE'RE NOT READY FOR THAT." "IT WON'T WORK IN THIS INDUSTRY." "THAT WILL MAKE OUR CURRENT SYSTEM OBSOLETE." "IT'S NOT PRACTICAL." "IT'S AGAINST THE RULES." "IT'S TOO REVOLUTIONARY." "OTHERS HAVE ALREADY TRIED THAT." "WE CAN'T SEE ANY SENSE IN IT." "THAT HASN'T BEEN PROVED YET." THOSE SAME PEOPLE, NOT LONG AGO, BELIEVED THE HUMAN BRAIN WAS A RADIATOR TO COOL THE BLOOD. THEY BELIEVED THE EARTH COULD NOT POSSIBLY BE A BALL BECAUSE THE PEOPLE ON THE BOTTOM WOULD FALL OFF. JUST TWENTY YEARS AGO A SCIENTIST WHO WOULD SPEAK OF SATELLITES WOULD HAVE COMMITTED ACADEMIC SUICIDE.

What we encounter here is the curious reinterpretation of history solely in the light of pragmatics; that is, the history of humankind is a history only of *homo faber*; there is no attention is paid to *homo sapiens* or *homo ludens*. Implicit in this, of course, is the acceptance of the scientific method as the only means of verification. And the last sentence contains an implicit evaluation of academia, the róle and purpose of the university.

NOTHING IS IMPROBABLE, IMPOSSIBLE, OR INCREDIBLE ANY LONGER.

Here we arrive at the ground of being, that which sustains our "confidence in the environment." Progress, what the above statement resolves to, is not only inevitable, but it is also transcendent. It stands not only beyond the possible, it stands beyond the probable and beyond the believable. It truly undergirds the whole of existence.

WHAT'S RIGHT WITH AMERICA, AND OTHER PEOPLE IN·

OTHER NATIONS ALSO, IS THAT AT LAST WE ARE
UNLOCKING THE REACH OF OUR MINDS, CASTING OFF
THE FEARS OF THE PAST, SEARCHING OUT FOR THE BEST
THAT IS IN US.

The "ugly American" epithet yields to that of the "anonymous
American"; this is to be understood in relation to the anonymous
Christian. There is no need to actively proselytize; others already
believe. We need simply make them explicitly aware of the faith they
implicitly profess.

WE LIVE IN AN EXCITING, CHALLENGING TIME. THE
EUPHORIA OF QUICK ANSWERS HAS PASSED. WE KNOW
WE SHALL NOT FIND A CANCER CURE IN THE
TWINKLING OF AN EYE, BUT WE SHALL FIND IT. LASTING
PEACE WILL NOT COME TOMORROW, BUT IT WILL
COME. RIGHT NOW, NOT SOME TIME IN THE FUTURE,
BUT RIGHT NOW TODAY, THE POSSIBILITIES FOR A
GOLDEN AGE EXIST. WE ARE MOVING, ACCOMPLISHING,
CHANGING, BUILDING ON THE BOLDEST SCALE IN
HUMAN HISTORY. SADLY, SO MANY PEOPLE DON'T SEE
THE WHOLE PICTURE, BUT ONLY WHAT THEY ARE
LOOKING AT. SO MANY SEE ONLY CHAOS.

The religion of science and technology must also come to grips
with the eschatological problem. For "golden age" read the
"kingdom of God." The tension between the *already here* and the *not
yet* is as problematic for this religion as it was (is) for the Christian
religion. The resolution achieved is not done by affirming that the
golden age exists now, nor that it will exist only at some time in the
future, but rather by affirming that "right now, today the
possibilities exist for the golden age." That is, the "whole picture"
includes the possibility for a golden age, not the actuality.

TRAGICALLY THE MEDIA ARE PASSING BY THEIR FINEST
OPPORTUNITY TO SERVE BY FAILING TO ACCOUNT FOR
THE AWESOME FORCES AT WORK TO BUILD A BETTER
WORLD. THE MEDIA OUGHT TO TAKE THE LEAD, TO
TRANSLATE WHAT'S HAPPENING. THEY OUGHT TO
TRANSMIT PRIDE, CONFIDENCE, ACHIEVEMENT. NOT
JUST TODAY, BUT IN WHERE AMERICA IS HEADING.

Unfortunately, the story continues, there are forces at work
against the needed faith view. Thus is introduced the theme of
dualism, the struggle between the forces of good (what's right with

America!'') and the forces of evil (those who "see only chaos").
AMERICANS HAVE DONE THEIR BEST BY TAKING THE
LEAD, BY ACTION, NOT CONVERSATION.

Besides the obvious reference to America as leader, once again we
encounter the pragmatic bent of this faith view. In theological terms
this is to insist on the primacy of works over faith, and of the active
life over the contemplative.
HISTORICALLY WE HUMANS HAVE LEFT THE DREAMING,
THE REAL THINKING AND DECISION MAKING TO A FEW.
NOW IT IS TIME TO TAKE THE REINS FROM THE FEW AND
INVEST DREAMING, THINKING, DECISION MAKING AND
ACTION WITH THE PEOPLE. CONVERTING INDIVIDUAL
POTENTIAL AND VISION INTO GLOBAL REALITY
EQUATES WITH A BRIGHT HORIZON OF PROGRESS.
WHAT'S RIGHT WITH AMERICA IS THAT AMERICA'S
HEARTBEAT IS GENERATED BY 214 MILLION FREE
PEOPLE. ADD TO THAT ANOTHER BILLION FREE OR
YEARNING TO BE FREE IN OTHER NATIONS AROUND THE
WORLD.

The salvific intent and scope of this faith view is universal: it is
not aristocratic, nor is it gnostic. It is meant for all people,
everywhere. This is the populist dimension which is so much a part
of it. This faith view, moreover, is ultimately what invests the entire
global reality with meaning. It is the one unifying force able to
transcend all ideological, political, cultural, religious and national
boundaries. Human life itself, all potentiality and vision, all
yearnings to be free, are taken up into the inevitable march of
progress.
COLLECTIVELY THE FREEDOM, THE KNOWLEDGE, THE
HUNGER TO SOLVE PROBLEMS PASSES ALL
COMPREHENSION AS THE MOST POWERFUL FORCE EVER
ASSEMBLED ON EARTH. OFF WITH THE SHACKLES OF
THE PAST. FOR SHAME THE GLOOM AND DOOM
MERCHANTS. THE FUTURE IS WHAT WE WILL CREATE. IT
IS FULL OF PROMISE.

The opening phrases ring of Paul's exclamation: "Oh, the
depths of the riches, the wisdom, etc." We have here a hymn to be
sung in the churches of progress, a song to its majesty. "The future is
what we will create. It is full of promise. Thus, concludes the story,
along with progress, there are two other catchwords which underpin

the pre-understanding of this faith view: future and promise.

It is the "future as promise" which constitutes the final referent for the story-myth of science and technology. In this we see already the tendency to forsake the present for the future. The future is where the real hope lies. This has always been the temptation to which apocalyptic thought is most susceptible; and it is no less the temptation facing science fiction as secular apocalyptic. For just as the present belongs to someone else (the traditionalists, conservationists, reactionaries, and environmentalists), so the future will belong to someone else (those who will reap the harvest of all our efforts). It is a no-win situation for the people who live now, caught up as they are in this time between the mess inherited from the past and the glorious future just around the corner.

Thus the nagging doubt, the terrible feeling that somehow the present generation is getting the short end of the stick. The "good old days" have passed them by, and the "good new days" have not yet arrived. The pendulum swings back and forth between nostalgia and frenzied activity in pursuit of the future which has been promised. Disillusionment reigns.

Yet the story continues to be told, and in that continued retelling it achieves an ersatz authority. It may not make sense of John Doe's life of quiet desperation in the face of increasing complexity, but it does make sense of the "whole picture." The story has a beginning (humankind separated itself from the animals to become *homo faber*), a middle (humankind continues to struggle in this role, in the face of the constant opposition from reactionaries), and an end (the future will see the struggle end when the promise is achieved). Who would not want to be a part of that story? Who would not want to look back on their life and say they have done their share to make it a reality? Who would not want to look forward and say: "I may not have had it so good, but, by damn, my children will!"

And out of the continued retelling a "religion" evolves. It possesses its own cult, ritual, language and ethic. It gradually and inexorably extends its meaning-giving power to more and more facets of life. It creates a monolithic structure of institutions, goals, practices, careers and thought patterns to resist the questions humankind has always asked: "Why does this exist? Why do the innocent suffer? Does the end ever justify the means? Who am I? What's it all about?"

Let us look briefly now at this religion of science and technology and explore some of its more obvious characteristics, especially as they are manifested in the stories of science fiction. This is premised on the fact that science fiction, as an apocalyptic literature, is written for believers. Those who are caught up in its faith world will understand. Again, a word of caution: This is not how all science and technology see themselves (although sometimes they do); this is how they are generally seen in the science fiction stories which are told and retold and become, in one sense, authoritative.

The central, all-inclusive myth of science and technology is PROGRESS. The underlying belief which flows from this myth is that progress is inevitable—not in itself, as some blind force, but in the efforts of humankind to overcome the obstacles nature places in its way. The referent of this myth is, as stated above, the future as promise.

All myths are cyclic in nature. (Perhaps this can somehow be related to the fact that time and space are curved realities, *a la* Einstein, but that is another whole matter.) Myths are cyclic because their function is to give meaning to the recurring thematic patterns of life. The agricultural myths are the epitome: the passage of the god(s) through death into the underworld and out again, is symbolic of the death of vegetation during winter and its rebirth in spring. Myths are always larger than life itself, dealing with birth, death and rebirth. They are populated with gods, with super-mortals, to signify their transcendence over the common, everyday occurrences and the individuals who inhabit the everyday world.

Myths do not go anywhere; that is, they do not treat of the resolution of time, history, world, life. The emergence of myths is not a step along the path of knowledge, signifying a dim comprehension of natural forces, to be surpassed later by a fuller understanding. Myths are timeless; not in the sense they endure, but in the sense that they include all of time within their confines. There is nothing new in myth; there is no unknown; there is no past, present or future. There is only the cycle.

Progress, as a myth, easily fits into the framework of this description. The inevitability of progress is mythic in its all-inclusiveness. As every spring is a rebirth in the agricultural myth, so in the technological myth every discovery, invention, innovation, change, improvement of product, procedure, or machine is progress. The inevitability of progress bestows a sacred meaning on all the activities of the technological person. This .mythic quality of progress, moreover, has nothing whatsoever to do with the past, present or future. There are no judgmental or evaluative comparisons to be made; it has no beginning or no end. Progress simply is. Jacques Ellu says of the "technique" underlying this myth of progress: "There is no purpose or plan that is progressively being realized. There is not even a tendency toward human ends. We are dealing with a phenomenon blind to the future, in a domain of integral causality."[1]

General Electric expressed most concisely the mythic quality of progress in its former slogan: "Progress is our most important product." The slogan has now been discarded; but not because of any re-evaluation of its inherent meaning, or disillusionment with its content. Progress as a word has simply fallen victim to the myth of progress. But progress as a myth was and is the foundation of all corporate endeavor and all technological dynamism in the world today.

Much of the science fiction written in the hey-day of the pulps is embued with the mythic quality of progress. The stories swallow up individuals with a much more voracious appetite than ever existed in any of the bug-eyed monsters. The mythic quality of progress is muted in much current science fiction, on the other hand; but it is there nonetheless. Whereas in early days technology and science triumphed over problems which resulted from outdated, inferior humanistic and romantic notions of reality, today technology and science are called upon to correct the wayward wanderings of science and technology themselves. While many present science fiction works purport to deal with the responsible use of technology in the creation of future, new heavens and earth, in reality they celebrate only the timelessness of progress. They have expanded the cycle, to be sure, to include many more dimensions of the complexity of human decisions, but they are still within the cycle.

The ritual of the myth of progress is RESEARCH AND DEVELOPMENT. The role of ritual in the socio-religious life of a people is to ensure the rebirth of the topocosm, the world of "this place," the immediate environment. Without a ritual to ensure rebirth, a people would perish. Through the ritual re-enactment of the dramatic elements of the myth, the continued fruitfulness of society (the topocosm) is ensured. The ritual, moreover, must participate in and give expression to all the characteristics of the myth. It must be cyclic (i.e., all-inclusive), timeless, and transcendent.

Research and development is the ritual of science and technology. It is all-inclusive insofar as it embraces all of life in its deliberations and analyses. There is nothing left outside its domain. Ellul writes in this regard that "technique" can be distinguished only according to the objects of study, not according to the means or the method used to study reality. He distinguishes three branches: economic technique, the technique of organization, and human technique. In the latter "man himself becomes the object of technique."[2] (In the current continual economic crisis, moreover, we see how, when technique is one for all branches, all the branches merge into one.)

Ritual and development is timeless in the sense that it does not exist in competition or comparison with anything past or future. It simply is. It lies outside the domain of any political, cultural, or ideological pattern of thought. It flourishes in dictatorships as well as in democracies. It responds to no basic human need; it exists only unto itself and for itself. It contains in its systems and conclusions no predetermined set of values or plan of action. In this latter characteristic it participates in the transcendent nature of the myth of progress. For research and development is the ritual re-enactment of the myth of the inevitability of progress. It bestows a sacred meaning on the "work" of the scientist and technician. Their role is to ensure the continued rebirth of the world as envisioned in the myth. If it were not for the myth of progress, there would be no need for the ritual of research and development. In turn, the ritual sustains the myth.

It may prove helpful to pause here and consider the relationship between science and technology; for it is at this point (when speaking of practical research and development) that scientists disassociate themselves from the horrors of technology. They claim that they are doing pure research. Ellul, when addressing this issue, always insists that what we should be talking about is "technique." Technique is prior to both science and the technology of machines. Yet all three are woven together. Although technique is prior to both historically, "to progress, technique had to wait for science."[3] Science needs technology to build laboratories; technique needs science to provide solutions to the problems it encounters. Through science, technique becomes ever more pervasive. Langdon Gilkey, to counter the argument of "pure" scientists that technicians are mere machinists, cites the writings of John Dewey, to the effect that the cognitive method of modern science underlies all technique, since it proposes to control data by intelligent foresight, and so be able to control the course of events. "Greater knowledge always means greater power," is Gilkey's aphorism.[4]

The ritual of research and development finds ample expression in the literature of science fiction—even though the research laboratories of the white-haired and white-smocked, benign and eccentric doctors, and their ravishingly beautiful daughters, are now, more often than not, replaced by the research facilities of a foundation or governmental agency, staffed by a hoard of specialists. Brian Aldiss, in his "true history" of science fiction, *Billion Year Spree*, argues that research laboratories and think tanks appear in science fiction long before they do in the world of government or corporation research and development. For the techological culture to survive far into the future (a billion years), there was needed the continuity of research laboratores, not the "random innovations of the solitary inventor." Even further, Aldiss argues, the pulp magazines themselves were the first think tanks, in which space travel was discussed and refined.[5]

There is, moreover, a pattern to the ritual. There are a thousand and one short stories and novels containing a plot which details the findings of pure research (conducted in the above described facilities) being taken over and subverted by evil persons (usually a military government or a dictator), turned against humankind, and then finally rescued and handed back to the people for their benefit. The parallel to the present defense industry is striking. The great apologist of technology, Buckminster Fuller, argues constantly that the research conducted for the military has accrued enormous benefits for humankind.

But even more striking are the parallels to the ancient rituals of birth, death and re-birth—the great cycle of the mythical world view. Research is born in the laboratory, dies in its misuse and/or subversion, and is reborn in its final application to the needs of humankind. The point is that many of the stories of science fiction are stories of the ritual re-enactment of the dramatic elements of the myth of the inevitability of progress. That myth says that ultimately research and development does benefit people; the topocosm will constantly be reborn in the struggle to free research from the designs of evil persons. The increasing appearance of dystopian versions of the ritual or research and development only underlines this message. For the warning taken mostly is that greater vigilance is needed, not that the research should be dropped. Thomas Disch's *Camp Concentration* and Ralph Blumm's *Simultaneous Man* are two such works, capable of an ambiguous reading on the matter of the ethics of pure research.

The language of science and technology is MATHEMATICS. It is the sacred language of the high priests, the scientists and technicians. As a sacred language, mathematics also participates in and gives expression to the characteristics of the myth of progress: it is all-inclusive, timeless, transcendent, and incapable of being misinterpreted. There is no double-think nor double-talk in its vocabulary or in its mental processes. To think and speak the sacred language of mathematics is to think and speak the truth. There is an inevitability present in mathematics which does not appear in other languages.

The sacred language of mathematics (insofar as it participates in and gives expression to the myth of progress and the ritual of research and development) lies at the heart of Isaac Asimov's *Foundation* trilogy. The concept of history contained therein is based on the language of mathematics. Apart from this, the trilogy is by and large a shallow social commentary; it is elitist, fascist, sexist and mercenary. It is an attempt to enshrine the gadget as god, and to remake the universe as Disneyland. It is only the language of the inevitability which saves the trilogy. Human history is reduced to the inevitability of progress. The understanding of that history is spoken in the language of mathematics, psycho-history:

> Psychohistory had been the development of mental science, the final mathematization thereof, rather, which had finally succeeded. Through the development of the mathematics necessary to understand the facts of neural physiology and the electro-chemistry of the nervous system, which themselves had to be, *had* to be, traced down to nuclear forces, it became first possible to truly develop psychology. And through the generalization of psychological knowledge from the individual to the group, sociology was also mathematicized.[6]

It is this mythic dimension of the *Foundation* trilogy which has created its mystique and perpetuated its popularity. For it embodies in the fullest the myth of progress, the ritual of research and development, and the sacred language of mathematics.

The ethics of science and technology is this: TO FASHION
THE ONE BEST POSSIBLE MEANS OF DOING. This is the
standard against which all technological innovation is measured.
Jacques Ellul says of technique that one of its principle
characteristics, if not *the* principle, is its "refusal to tolerate moral
judgments." He goes on to say:

Technique never observes the distinction between moral and immoral use. It
tends, on the contrary, to create a completely independent technical morality
.... Technique pursues no end, professed or unprofessed. It evolves in a
pure causal way: the combination of preceeding elements furnishes the new
technical elements. There is no purpose or plan that is being progressively
realized.[6]

There is inherent in the ethic of science and technology an
insistence on its all-inclusiveness; this it shares with the myth of
progress, the ritual of research and development, and the sacred
language of mathematics. The ethic says that science and technology
cannot be judged by anything outside their domain. The "can"
becomes the "ought"; the categorical imperative of Kant is
transformed into the technological imperative; "It was possible,
therefore it was necessary." The introduction of the "ought" (or
"must") signals the realm of ethics. But this is the ethics of
instrumentality, not of responsibilty. As if to underline this fact, and
tie the ethic of science and technology in with the myth of progress
and the ritual of research and development, Ellul argues that one
consequence of technical autonomy is that it "renders technique at
once sacrilegious and sacred."[8] By this he means that technique has
on the one hand destroyed the sacred mystery of life, but on the other
hand replaced it with the ritual of research and development.

The ethic of "the one best possible means" manifests itself in the
incessant claims made for this object, process or procedure as being
the "best, fastest, highest, biggest, most beautiful, most efficient,
most economical," and so forth. The relationship of technique to the
marketplace is not accidental. Progress has created an over-
abundance. This, and not the depletion of natural resources, is the
immediate problem facing us. This in turn means that economic
control gives way to social control. The marketplace no longer
controls, but rather is controlled by the giant corporation through
the medium of advertising. Increased productivity feeds on increased
demand, suggesting that one must produce the demand as well as the

product. In the straight-thinking world of John W. Campbell, Jr., the "father" of the Golden Age of Science Fiction, there is no problem here: planned obsolescence is a necessity. "American devices are built generally on the basis that a good unit is one which will serve faithfully until the better unit now in the research stage gets into production."[9]

The classic dystopian vision of the ultimate bankruptcy of the ethic of the one best possible means is *The Space Merchants* by Frederick Pohl and C.M. Kornbluth. It is classic for the very reason that it explores the relationship between advertising and technology. The tangled dimensions of the relationship are embodied in the designation so often given to the person caught in between: the consumer. Along with the nuclear bomb, today's symbol for humankind as both victim and executioner is the consumer. In the world of *The Space Merchants* the advertising agencies are the corporate-conglomerates of the universe; they control everything, from resources to government. The price the people must pay is consumption; and the means of slavery is, literally, addiction:

But—and here's what makes this campaign truly great, in my estimation—each sample of Coffiest contains three milligrams of a simple alkaloid. Nothing harmful. But definitely habit-forming. After ten weeks the customer is hooked for life. It would cost him at least five thousand dollars for a cure, so it's simpler for him to go right on drinking Coffiest—three cups with every meal and a pot beside his bed at night, just as it says on the jar.[10]

The Space Merchants was published in 1953.

Thus briefly the myth, ritual, language and ethics standing behind science fiction—when the task is to lay clear the "faith" implicit in this secular apocalyptic world view. This faith is not the way it really is. It does not leap out at the reader from every page, beating him or her into submission. But very quietly it works its subtleties, until finally it becomes the "way it ought to be." Indeed, the way it will be. This is the vision according to which the future will unfold, in these terms, with this understanding, guided largely by the unspoken assumptions of the "faith" which both writer and reader bring to the story, describing a future which cannot be known in the same way the present is known.

There is no one definite, common vision of the future; but there emerges, through an analysis of the stories of science fiction, a common, definite method of thinking about and imagining the future. This is critical for an understanding of an apocalyptic world view; it is the basis for a hope shared in the present—a hope that tomorrow will see it beginning to happen. This hope needs to be affirmed and confirmed over and over, for it, in turn, is the implicit basis of meaning for the very work and life of the believer in his or her everyday activity.

When we turn, now, to another look at the stories of science fiction, it is with this in mind: to explore further the dynamic of this faith as it operates through symbol and image. In addition we gain further insight into the centrality of story.

In terms of our present discussion, science fiction is secular apocalyptic literature which seeks to give hope. It is written to comfort those disillusioned with the failure of the promise of science and technology, specifically, to deliver the world today from poverty, ignorance, disease, war, famine, plague and death. On this level science fiction can be seen as responding to an historical crisis, which is also a crisis of faith, by providing the stories, symbols, images and myths needed to help cope with that crisis.

The particular, detailed facets of the crisis, however, are as varied as are the stories and styles of science fiction. There is no one scenario of a crisis which alone symbolically represents the "imagery of death and technological annihilation" which Lifton claims haunts our waking lives. Every cluster of symbols and images presents a different facet of the crisis. Some of these I would now like to explore. My working thesis, very simply put, is that through myth, image and symbol science fiction treats of the meanings, values and problematic areas of life incapable of being dealt with satisfactorily on the conceptual level; that is, as clear and distinct ideas able to be manipulated systematically. The reason in part for the resurgence of apocalyptic imagery is that we need some kind of statement about the future, yet we cannot validly make scientific statements about a reality which is not empirically observable. Thus the need for every story and symbol. Another reason for the resurgence is that statements of science and technology invariably appear to us to be cold and impersonal; they invite no personal response. Conceptually they can provide understanding; but they cannot provide what is radically needed: meaning.

Of recent, more and more anthropologists, philosophers and theologians have been calling for the reintroduction of the symbolic dimension into the understanding of human values. The secular scientific world view, when it remains on the conceptual level, lacks the language to thematize the experience of the ultimate which is at the core of everyday life. But as soon as it moves to the symbolic level, it touches base. At this level it operates to give meaning to daily experience. Allow me to cite the analysis of Jacques Ellul as a case in point.

Among the laws of technique which Ellul explicates is the law of self-augmentation. The law is twofold: "1) In a given civilization, technical progress is irreversible. 2) Technical progress tends to act, not according to arithmetic, but according to geometric progression."[11] Now, increase according to geometric progression is also one of the laws of population growth. When this symbolic link is made, then we realize that at the heart of the myth of science lie the fertility rites which ensure the continued fruitfulness of technological innovation—specifically, the rebirth of the new creation as robots, new energy sources, space travel, computers, and so forth. In other words, it is possible to analyze the law of self-augmentation by studying the fertility rites and myths surrounding them, and not simply by remaining on the conceptual level, where Ellul remains.

This is much more valuable when making connections with science fiction, since the latter is also story, which has become myth.

The rites of revitalization and re-invigoration in ancient societies are for all practical purposes synonymous with the fertility rites of those same societies. An integral part of many fertility rites in agricultural societies involved the tribal leader/national king ritually entering the temple to have sexual intercourse with the temple prostitute. The symbolic ritual act ensured the fertility of the earth in spring. These ritual acts took place in ancient Rome, on the Ides of March, among the Piples of Central America, in Java, and among the Hereros of Central America. And even today, it is said, in parts of the Ukraine, married couples have intercourse in the fields on St. George's day, April 23, to ensure a fertile season.[12] Robert Silverberg picks up on this motif in his *A Time for Changes*; but he cannot help himself in later debunking the "mythic" dimensions of the ritual act. The reason people sow the fields while naked is that they thereby do away with the bother of washing the clothes of the sowers who slip and fall in the mud.

There is ample evidence in the Bible to substantiate the claim that one of the major temptations and failures of the Israelite people involved their participation in the fertility rites of the local religions. This theme runs all the way through the Bible, from the serpent in the garden (a symbol of fertility), through the prophets' castigations of the people for seeking out the temple prostitutes, to the battle in the Apocalypse of John against the great primeval serpent (traced back to the garden) and the river of life (God's fertility) which runs through the New Jerusalem.

To the present day, the charge of unfaithfulness carries along with it this dimension of biblical thought. Israel was constantly being reprimanded for having "prostituted themselves to other gods." Some biblical commentators may regard this as a customary figure of speech for idol worship; but it is in reality the working symbol for a large part of the Old Testament. Hosea, moreover, was commanded by God to take as his wife a prostitute, and to love her. This was a symbol of what it is like for God to love his people, who have continually played the prostitute. A counter theme running through the Bible at the same time presents the desert as being the truly fertile land. It is the desert which gives birth to the Israelite nation and the Jesus/Messiah; the desert is also the locale for the writing of a portion of the Bible itself—the Apocalypse of John is said to have been written on a desert isle. The symbol implies that it is God who is the final source of fertility.

Marshall McLuhan, in *Understanding Media*, underscores the parallels between the fertility rites of ancient societies and those of technological society. He speaks often of humankind's relationship to technology in sexual overtones. The closest example at hand is the automobile. The slang phrase, "hot rod," is the working symbol in this analysis. But the symbolism always points to a deeper reality. The car needs a driver as much as the person needs a car. Indeed, the machine needs the human on a much more profound level than the human needs the machine, for humankind is the servo-mechanism of the machine. The need extends all the way down to the level of the machine's continued existence—that is, its survival, the primary instinct, the instinct to reproduce the species. McLuhan thus writes: "Man becomes, as it were, the sex organs of the machine world, as the bee of the plant world, enabling it to fecundate and to evolve ever newer forms. The machine world reciprocates man's love by expediting his wishes and desires, namely, in providing him wealth."[13] For some the relationship is not quite so reciprocal. Arthur C. Clarke has argued in effect that it is impossible for the IBM computer to have evolved without having first gone through the biological phase.[14]

The image of humankind as the bee that fertilizes the technological topocosm is one which McLuhan may have borrowed from Buckminster Fuller, the apologist for technology. Fuller writes:

All biological life has its built-in drives by virtue of which various species make unwitting contributions to other species and thus to the total success of all biological life. Thus, for instance, do the bees, intent only upon their built-in drive for honey, inadvertently cross-fertilize vegetation by inter-dusting the vitalizing pollens with their carelessly bumbling tails. In somewhat the same relationship to the total success of a totally industrializing world man's ecology, the trade union organizers—intent only on getting their better wages and shorter hours for their dues-paying members—have also inadvertently spread the guaranteed purchasing capability to such larger numbers of the public as to justify the banking systems' extending loans for multiyears which have altogether made possible mass production and mass distribution of ever larger and costlier and more scientifically-prototyped end products and services.[15]

The passage comes from Fuller's *Utopia or Oblivion*. Without commenting on how Fuller sets up the option, one need only point out that his analysis fits in quite well with the understanding of ritual as research and development.

Jacques Ellul himself uses an example other than the fertilizing bee, but he makes the same point about humankind's relationship to technology—and with surprisingly similar sexual overtones. "Man," Ellul writes, "is reduced to the level of a catalyst. Better still he resembles a slug inserted into a slot machine; he starts the operation without participating in it."[16] One is here reminded of the common designation of electrical components as male/female. In this regard, it can be noted that "communion" in Jack Williamson and Frederick Pohl's *Star Child* is achieved by "plugging into" the central computer—an image which finds its way into an increasing number of science fiction stories.

The fertility rites of the technological myth also make clear another point, very important in our day: *the proliferation of technology is the population bomb of the new creation.* Reproduction of the machine (breathing life into it) is a function that humankind has reserved to itself—in much the same manner that "God" has reserved the creation of life to him/herself. The result is that the machine feels no responsibility to limit its own propulation/productivity.

Sociologists, philosophers, and theologians are finally beginning to wrestle with this problem of the proliferation of technology and its population bomb on a conceptual level. But the writers of science fiction have treated it symbolically almost from the very beginning—most forcefully when writing about robots. Karl Capek, the Czechoslovakian writer who "invented" the robot (at least the name), wrestled with the question in 1923. In his play *R.U.R.* the robots achieve power by beginning to kill off people. At the end, however, they plead with the one remaining person left in the world; for they need his assistance in discovering the secret to the process of reproduction. Failing to learn it, they realize, they will become extinct.

Succeeding science fiction has resolved this question by giving humankind the power of life and death over the machine; for it is humankind who reproduces the machine, either electronically/mechanically in the robot/computer, or chemically in the android. The power of humankind over the android, however, has increasingly been challenged—most intelligently, sympathetically and strongly in Clifford D. Simak's *Time and Again*. In Arthur C. Clarke's *Childhood's End*, on the other hand, there exists a commentary on the relationship between humankind and its technology which will serve as a concluding statement. The Overlords in this book act as midwives, being dispatched around the universe by the Overmind to assist at the delivery of new para-mental and para-psychological beings. They themselves cannot reproduce, nor share in the powers who come into being. They exist only to serve, both the Overmind and the particular race to whom they are sent. It is this precise relationship where humankind finds itself today—sterile, yet assisting at the · birth of awesome, new technological marvels which have been created, not by humankind, but by technology and science itself. Technology may be self-augmenting, but it needs humankind as the mid-wife. Clarke's description of the pathos of the situation in which the Overlords find themselves could well be applied to the human race:

So this, thought Jan, with a resignation that lay beyond all sadness, was the end of man. It was an end that no prophet had ever foreseen—an end that repudiated optimism and pessimism alike.[17]

The symbolism of technology as the "extensions of man," popularized extensively by McLuhan, affords yet another opportunity to explore science and technology as a religious phenomenon. Fuller lays the groundwork and McLuhan expands on it: The media are the extensions of humankind, insofar as technology extends the senses and/or motor activities of the human race. At the same time, however, sense perceptions are altered by the very extensions themselves, and by the interaction and interconnection of the perceptive sense organs. "The medium is the message," McLuhan wrote, in his most quotable aphorism—to underline the alteration effected by those extensions. To be in constant touch, for example, with the whole world through electronic media is itself the message that the world is a global village. One does not have to add to it the statement that the world is a global village.

But McLuhan spends much more time on, and gives far deeper consideration to the interconnection and interaction of the sensory organs and the central nervous system itself. He begins by talking about the myth of Narcissus as an example of "sense closure," not as an example of self love. The image which Narcissus saw has this effect: it closes him off to other incoming sensory data. Any one, intense sensory experience will do the same. Dentists often use high intensity sound to block out pain; we turn down the radio to concentrate on trying to see something; we turn off the television to listen; we shut our eyes to a loud noise.

Technology, McLuhan argues, is a successive series of intense sensory experiences which close us off. The final and most far-reaching of these has been the electronic media, for they are extensions of the central nervous system itself. In response to this bombardment, we have become numb; we are relatively unaffected by other data. McLuhan cites Psalm 115 to explore his point:

> . . . their idols, in silver and gold,
> products of human skill
> have mouths but never speak
> eyes but never see
> ears but never hear
> noses but never smell
> hands but never touch
> feet but never walk
> and not a sound from their throats.
> Their makers will end up like them
> and so will anyone who relies on them.

He then continues his analysis by arguing that the concept of "idol" for the Hebrew mentality is similar to that of the myth of Narcissus for the Greek mentality. For the psalmist argues that the very looking at and/or worshipping of the idols will conform humankind to them. The same is true of technology. McLuhan writes: "By continually embracing technologies, we relate ourselves to them as servomechanisms. That is why we must, to use them at all, serve these objects, these extensions of ourselves, as gods or minor religions."[18]

Humankind continues to create its gods. The very explicit message of Clifford D. Simak's *A Choice of Gods* is precisely this point. After the burden of technology has been lifted from the remnant left behind on earth (the others have departed to follow the universal mind), longevity of life ensures, along with telepathy and mental transportation. We can choose the gods who serve our material needs, or we can choose those who serve our spiritual, psychic needs. There is, however, no choice about the necessity of choosing gods.

The operative symbols for the idol in the Apocalypse of John are the dragon and the beast. The great dragon is in reality the primeval serpent. This again reminds us of the fertility rites, and the ultimate questions concerning the author of life and the tactics of survival, that is, our salvation. The relationship of humankind to the dragon and the beast is one of worship and service. But now we can begin to explore this relationship in terms of what was said above about fertility rites. Behind whatever beast may appear there is always the dragon. Thus we read in the Apocalypse of John:

They prostrated themselves in front of the dragon because he had given the beast his authority; and they prostrated themselves in front of the beast, saying, "Who can compare with the beast? How can anybody defeat him?" (Rev. 13:4)

One obvious referent for the beast in our own time is the military machine, precisely because it is among the most technologically oriented sectors of our society. It is efficient if it is nothing else. We read further:

It worked great miracles, even to calling down fire from heaven on to the earth while people watched. Through the miracles which it was allowed to do on behalf of the first beast, it was able to win over the peoples of the world and persuade them to put up a statue in honor of the beast that had been wounded by the sword and still lived. It was allowed to breathe life into this statue, so that the statue of the beast was able to speak, and to have anyone who refused to worship the statue of the beast to be put to death. He compelled everyone, small and great, rich and poor, slave and citizen, to be branded on the right hand or on the forehead, and made it illegal for anyone to buy or sell anything unless he had been branded with the name of the beast or the number of its name. (Rev. 13:13-17)

But behind the beast is always the dragon; there is more to the military machine than mere efficiency. It is always fertility which is worshipped—and technology is fertile if it is nothing else. No matter how destructive of life it is ultimately, it is clung to and worshipped as that which gives life. Thus, in this case, warfare ensures peace, arms production creates jobs, and the army builds men! The beast serves the dragon.

The operative symbol for the idol as the technological extension of humankind in science fiction is Frankenstein. The passage of time has merged the "monster" of Frankenstein with Frankenstein himself. This is no accident; it is simply the working of sense closure, as McLuhan would say, or of "becoming like unto them," as the psalmist would have it. It simply means that Frankenstein has become as much the monster as the monster is merely an image of its creator.

The hard-core science fiction creature of the laboratory is, of course, the robot. Much has been made of the fact that robots (mechanical, electronic, or chemical) are no longer Frankensteins; or at least, given half a chance, they will not inevitably turn out that way. *Adam Link*, by Eando Binder, is among the most simplistic science fiction presentations of this rationale. The name for the robot, "Adam" for the first man, and "Link" for the missing link, presumably ought to tip us off that this is an impossible mish-mash of scientific and theological evolutionary romanticism. *Adam Link* is an early science fiction work; but other early examples abound giving vent to a similar vein of romanticism. Among the more notable is the short story "Helen O'Loy," by Lester del Rey, in which, far from being a monster, the created robot becomes the perfect domestic and sexual partner. Science fiction is often thinly disguised wish-fulfillment.

The romanticism surrounding early stories of robots gives way eventually to a logical and rational treatment of their place in a technological society. Thus is Frankenstein finally and wholly subsumed into humankind. The person to whom most credit is due in overcoming the Frankenstein image of robots and computers is Isaac Asimov. Famous indeed are Asimov's three "Laws of Robotics," imprinted into the robot's positronic brain:

1.) A robot may not injure a human being, or, through inaction allow a human being to come to harm.
2) A robot must obey the orders given it by human beings except where such orders would conflict with the First Law.
3) A robot must protect its own existence as long as such protection does not conflict with the First or Second Law.[19]

The achievement of Asimov is that he has created not only a new being, but a new way of being. The robot is no longer set over against humankind; now the machine becomes man and man becomes the machine, through the use of reason and through adherence to the three laws of robotics. One can see this progression clearly in the stories which make up Asimov's book, *I, Robot*. In the story "Reason," for example, the following incident takes place:

"I have spent these last two days in concentrated introspection," said Cutie, a robot, "and the results have been most interesting. I began at one sure assumption I felt permitted to make. I, myself, exist, because I think—".... "And the question that immediately rose was: Just what is the cause of my existence?"
Powell's jaw set lumpily. "You're being foolish. I told you already that we made you." ...
The robot spread its strong hands in a depreciatory gesture, "I accept nothing on authority. A hypothesis must be backed by reason, or else it is worthless—and it goes against all dictates of logic to suppose that you made me."[20]

In "Evidence" a virtual man/machine, Stephen Byerly, is running for mayor of a large city. Because of the still residual fear of robots (the Frankenstein myth) he cannot allow this fact to be known—that he is indeed a robot. But Dr. Susan Calvin, chief robopsychologist, makes the following comments:

"If a robot can be created capable of being a civil executive, I think he'd make the best one possible. By the Laws of Robotics, he'd be incapable of tyranny, of corruption, of stupidity, of prejudice. And after he had served a decent term he would leave, even though he were immortal, because it would be impossible for him to hurt humans by letting them know that a robot had ruled them. It would be most ideal."

"Except that a robot might fail due to the inherent inadequacies of his brain. The positronic brain has never equalled the complexities of the human brain."

"He would have advisors. Not even a human brain is capable of governing without advisors."[21]

The robots have not yet made it to the final level, where they have achieved superiority over human beings. But at least they have reduced humankind into talking their language. No longer is it a human being, a bundle of thoughts, feelings, emotions, hunches and pig-headedness, who governs; it is the human brain which governs. Once humankind begins to use this kind of language, it can no longer resist the march toward the "evitable conflict." This is the title of the final story, wherein humankind has reached its limit, wherein it realizes that humankind cannot even become like unto its idol—for the robots have far outstripped them. They rule the world, but of course for humankind's benefit. Dr. Calvin admits that "perhaps robotists as a whole should now die, since we no longer understand our own creations." Nevertheless, she concludes:

"How do we know what the ultimate good of Humanity will entail? We haven't at *our* disposal the infinite factors that the Machine has at *its*! .... We don't know. Only the Machines know, and they are going there and taking us with then."

"But you are telling me, Susan, that ... Mankind *has* lost its own say in its future."

"It never really had any. It was always at the mercy of economic and sociological forces that it did not understand—at the whims of the climate, and the fortunes of war. Now the Machines understand them; and no one can stop them, since the Machines will deal with them as they are dealing with society—having as they do the greatest weapons at their disposal, the absolute control of our economy."

"How horrible!"

"Perhaps how wonderful! Think, that for all time, all conflicts are finally evitable. Only the Machines, from now on, are inevitable."[22]

The roboticists may no longer understand their creation, but anyone else can see that they are readily understandable—for the robots have been made in our own image, instilling them with the use of reason, and filling their brains with the three laws of robotics. In the end we have become like unto them.

The symbolism of robots in Asimov's *I, Robot* and in much

other science fiction treating of robots, operates on at least four different levels. On the first level, the question is raised: In whose image are we made? How do we speak of God creating us? On the second level, the whole question is transposed over into our "creation" of the robots, who now have their own identity and personality. And with whom we can only interact on their level. On the third level the question becomes: Who serves whom? And on the fourth level, far removed it seems, but really at the heart of the matter, is the fact of sense closure—the fact that robots/machines do not rule by domination but by satisfying our every need, while at the same time creating those needs. When the system has closed in upon itself, it becomes so much more easy to serve the beast and worship the dragon.

Even further, what the three laws of robotics signify is that technology can exclude the strange, the tragic, the unplanned for, and the evil of chance from the world. Perhaps this is why Ellul is so insistent upon the use of the word "technique" rather than technology in his analysis of the technological society. He wants to make it clear that it is not the metal, glass, plastic and electronic objects which make up the technological society; it is rather the carefully rationalized plans of action, whose intent is to fashion an artificial world, which really embody the mystique of technology. It is the morality of instrumentality, rather than the morality of responsibility, which characterizes the technological era. The hope of the technological society is precisely for the "evitable conflict."

Apocalyptic literature, however, is a terrifying reminder that such hopes are illusory; it is more likely the inevitable conflict which waits for us down the road of history. Yet even here the symbols and their messages are confusing. To return to an earlier analysis, the question remains: Is it life after death? Or is it life over death? This is the crisis which the bomb foments in our society, and in the stories of science fiction.

The crisis precipitated by the bomb is perhaps the most well chronicled crisis of our times. For the bomb has given us a handle on doomsday—the ultimate fear. Small consolation that handle may be; yet when joined with the guided missile, the cluster of symbols suddenly achieves a prominence hard to surpass. This cluster of symbols, bomb/guided missile/doomsday, stands at once for the day of judgment and the day of deliverance. There is really no other way to understand the suicidal rush toward doomsday witnessed to in the nuclear arms race. Doomsday is devoutly to be wished for, and strongly to be feared. The vengeance of divine judgment is surpassed only by the vengeance of human judgment—as plan after plan is formulated for bombing the enemy into oblivion. The cluster of symbols is both the end of everything and the beginning of a new era. Time after time, from the radioactive ashes of an obliterated earth, the survivors rise up to rebuild the new earth. There is no thought given to the fact that they carry with them the seeds of their own eventual destruction in the libraries they preserve. The bomb, further, unites us in our fear and dependency; yet it divides us in our bomb shelters. The "survival of the fittest" ideology undermines all our instincts for community and the sentiments of fellowship. Bob Dylan, as pointed out above, sings continuously in his early songs about the divisive nature of fall-out shelters. Yet it is precisely this which is to be carried over into the new world.

On the other hand, it is argued, the bomb/guided missile/doomsday cluster of symbols pushes us over the brink of animality and guides us toward true responsibilty. Commentators there are who argue that, pushed as we are to the brink, scientists and technicians among us, along with military planners, have rediscoverd their morality and humanity. Yet too often it is the morality of brinksmanshihp, or the morality of individual conversion in the face of imminent doom. An oft-cited example of this is Mordecai Roshwald's *Level 7*. One can applaud the conversion of the protagonist, who sits deep within the bowels of the earth at the very end of civilization. But what else is left as the whole thing collapses? What "right" does he have to be loving and caring in such circumstances? The "life after death" of private conversion finds its perfect setting in the "life after death" nature of the bomb shelter.

Others have argued that the guided missile is the phallic symbol, both of our power to conquer and dominate and of our impotencey to be loving and caring. If this be so, then pushing the button is the ultimate example of masturbation. The symbol can also be used when speaking of the rocket ship "conquering" space—the virgin frontier. Finally, the cluster of bomb/guided missile/doomsday is the work of Cain; henceforth we are both the victim and the executioner. The crisis precipitated by this cluster means that the "future as promise" is present most forcefully in its negation.

The very ambiguity evoked by the bomb/guided missile/doomsday cluster of symbols signifies, in effect, that a new

understanding of humankind is emerging. In perhaps one of the
most perceptive evocations of this new understanding, J.G. Ballard
writes of *homo eniwetok*. It is the story of a man who goes back to the
tiny atoll in the Pacific, Eniwetok, on which the last atmospheric test
of the hydrogen bomb took place. His goal is to discover just who he
is. The name of the short story, "The Terminal Beach," suggests that
he is both the first and the last of his kind. Technological man has
discovered his own mortality: gone forever is the naive romanticism
of *I, Robot*. David Ketterer, who generally discounts the
mythological function of much science fiction, does admit the
validity of claiming that the "terminal beach" is one myth to which
science fiction can lay claim. The myth says that just as humankind
emerged as a possibility when life moved from the sea onto land, so
the denouement of humankind will take place on the same beach.
Ketterer traces the origin of this myth from H.G. Wells' "The Star"
through Nevil Shute's *On the Beach*, to Ballard's short story from
whence comes the name of the myth, and the name for the new
humanity.[23]

There are many other science fiction works which treat of this
cluster of symbols; some will be discussed in later chapters. Here I
will conclude by mentioning only one: Doris Lessing's *The Four-
Gated City*. Lessing is (was) known as a mainstream writer, depicting
in her novels the deep anxieties afflicting our age. In this novel of life
in London during the "Ban the Bomb" demonstrations, the spectre
of the bomb haunts the lives and souls of all the characters. It is no
surprise that one of them takes to writing "space fiction," as she calls
it. Nor is it a surprise that Lessing herself, in the final section of the
novel, speculates about the immediate future (the next 60 to 70 years),
in which commune-city states are set up in remote places of the earth,
pending the inevitable conflict, and in which people gradually
develop para-psychological powers. The "mutations" are already
taking place, the story says. Because of the very presence of the bomb,
a new understanding and a new mode of human existence is coming
into being. To have built the bomb is already to have pushed the
button.

This last point is recognized in the fact that theoreticians
themselves admit the failure of purely conceptual knowledge to
convey the meaning of the technological age. They usually engage in
the writing of scenarios of possible futures, in order to understand
just what they are up against and what new plans have to be

fashioned. This witnesses to the fact that the cold, calculating language of science and technology fails to evoke the dimensions of human existence at which only story, symbol and myth can get. We will explore two further symbols in the following chapter, the city and doomsday.

CHAPTER THREE

THEMATIC SYMBOL ANALYSIS affords almost unlimited opportunities for the student of science fiction. But it can become a dead end, leading away from confrontation with the critical dimension of the apocalyptic imagination: temporality and historical consciousness. The hope which apocalyptic confirms and consoles makes sense only in reference to actual historical life. Apocalyptic arises in the context of a historical crisis and it seeks to illuminate that crisis, shedding light on the question of how it is that life can possibly come out of (this) death. Myth also, since it is timeless and cyclical, ultimately shies away from speaking of the end—in linear images. In myth there is only cycle within cycle—or, as is so often the case in science fiction, the opposite holds true: there is only cycle outside of cycle, as the farthest reaches of space and time are explored. Progress gives way only to further progress. And sequel to sequel.

There is no real story, however, without an end. Here McLuhan's dictum applies: The medium is the message. Story itself is the message; and end of (to) the story becomes the final illuminating feature, clarifying all that has gone before. Frank Kermode's book *The Sense of an Ending* and Ray L. Hart's statement that "Life is lived from the end," are best understood insofar as they relate to the stories we tell about the end. For in those stories is revealed, not so much our goals and dreams but our historical consciousness, our awareness not only of what will come to pass but also of how it will come to pass. To begin our exploration of the topic, two themes in science fiction, the city and doomsday, need to be looked at.

"Diaspar is the archetypal science-fiction city," says Gary K. Wolfe, in commenting on Arthur C. Clarke's *The City and the Stars.* He continues: "It stands in the midst of the unknown just as humanity exists in the wilderness of space and time, and its wonder comes not only from the implication of the waste beyond, but also from the awe at what might be accomplished with human knowledge."[1]

The words of another literary critic might be applied to Diaspar:

[It] resists translation into any terms other than the ones intrinsic to itself and can therefore be regarded as immune to the general breakdown of taste and cultivation around it .... [it] helps ensure continuity and integrity of civilization by retaining its character as a non-referential, autotelic, self-sufficient object, a kind of self-enclosed garden with no relation to the modern turbulence and confusion outside.[2]

The similarities in description only serve to highlight the discrepancy in referent. For, while Wolfe is speaking of the archetypal science fiction city, Giles Gunn, in the second passage, is caricaturing how the "objective orientation" in modern literary criticism views the literary object: to be studied and analyzed as an organic unity, incapable of being translated into terms other than the ones intrinsic to itself, immune to extrinsic chaos, and indeed having the weakest of connections to that external turbulence. The ease with which one can interchange the art form of the city and the art form of the literary object, with scarcely a loss of meaning, suggests that it is as easy to misread the city as it is to misread literature.

The point which Gunn argues in his essay is that "literature is less a spatial than a temporal art."[3] But this holds as well for the city. The overriding tendency in the study of the past and the planning of future cities is to read the city itself as a spatial art form, and consequently to locate its meaning in its existence as "non-referential, autotelic, self-sufficient, self-enclosed," that is, as existing in a "wilderness of space and time." Such is the idealized city conceived by humankind, planned and projected in utopian literature, from Plato's *Republic* and More's *Utopia*, to Bellamy's *Looking Backward* and Skinner's *Walden Two*, and the hundreds of future cities of contemporary science fiction. All such projections rely heavily on the city as a spatial art form: nothing but the self-enclosed city is needed to understand the city.

Against this tendency (which can be called the image of the city as utopia) stands the city as temporal image, symbolic of the historicity of humankind, having a beginning, a process of coming into being, and an end. In this symbolic language, the city projected as the New Jerusalem is not the city as utopia, but the city as apocalyptic. Viewed less as a spatial image and more as a temporal image, the city tells the story of the growth and development of humankind. When one tells the story of the city, or listens to its tale, there transpires a critical ordering of one's responses through which is elicited, to use again the words of Gunn, "a re-alignment of the affections, a reordered sense of value, a new disposition of the heart."[4]

To read the city as a temporal image, then, is not to seek to reorder our space, but our time, our beginnings and our ends, and most importantly of all, our coming into being. This, it seems to me, is the dynamism of the image of the city as apocalyptic. The result is that the basic polarity is not between the utopian and the dystopian city, but between the city seen as utopian and the city seen as apocalyptic. The polarity, I trust, will be the occasion for dialectic, not judgment.

But let us backtrack briefly at this point, to specify the terms of our discussion so that the reading of the city as apocalyptic is continuous with our reading of apocalypse as apocalyptic.

Apocalypse reveals; its form is its function. It is story in the form of ecstatic vision, dream, discourse cycle, moral exhortation—all in various combinations, or none exactly. In the discussion above we listed some of the more common literary and stylistic features, their meaning and their function. I want now to introduce another feature, relate it to our discussion of the city, and do some initial reflections on how it functions in the Apocalypse of John.

Apocalypse functions as a recapitulative coda of scripture. Although the usual impulse is to interpret recapitulation as a summary of all that has gone before, this is to miss its revelatory dimension. Recapitulation does not just reveal *what* happened, but *how* it came to happen. For our purposes, not what we are, but how we came to be. It does not only inform, it truly reveals; for revelation is the rendering of humankind present to itself in subjective appropriation, whereas information stands as objective data, unable to transform the subject. Recapitulation reveals, for it makes all things present and says that we cannot step away from our past, we cannot divorce ourselves from our process of coming into being.

In apocalypse the forms of recapitulation vary, but the usual means are the great surveys of history: the descriptions of ages past, the present age, and the age to come. Since the date of composition of these surveys is deliberately shifted, there is ambiguity about what is past and what is future history in apocalypse. Thus the revelation is that we are what we have been and what we will be, we live always in the time of transition, of judgment, of renewals. We live always at the critical time, the turning point, the hinge. The past as well as the present and the future depends on our faith and trust in God's saving action. For he is God of the living, not the dead.

The Apocalypse of John illustrates graphically the recapitulative dimension of apocalyptic literature. If I may borrow the biological dictum, "Ontogeny recapitulates phylogeny," the case can then be stated as follows: The Apocalypse of John traces the development of the phylum (the chosen people) through the development of the individual (the Lamb, Jesus). It thus recapitulates what has happened (will happen) to the chosen people through a portrayal of the Lamb's victory over the beast.

We have here more than a summary of what has transpired in the past, or what will transpire in the future; more than a table of contents or an outline of history. We have, in short, a story about the story of humankind, a revelation not only of what we are, but of how we came to be born in the fullness of our being, without a short-circuiting of history. I might add that to read recapitulation as plan, and not as story, will result in that short-circuiting. Story allows for controlled feedback (it pauses for laughter and applause, sidetracks for detail and explanation), while plan does not—it overloads and breaks down. One could say that the major sin committed in reading the Apocalypse of John is reading it as plan, not story. Thus from Joachim of Fiore on, the "Three Ages" has become the plan for forcing God's intervention into history.[5]

If there is one symbol central to both the Apocalypse of John and the bulk of science fiction, illustrating in a most striking manner the revelatory dimension of recapitulation, it is the city. Nor is the use of the city in such a manner limited to biblical hermeneutics. Historians, cultural anthropologists, and philosophers all agree that to study the history of the city is to study world history. Even in the present developmental processes of the city, however, there is seen in kernel, in seed, in embryo all the life and history of the human race. Edmund Bacon calls the city a "form determining process,"[6] which is to say nothing other than ontogeny recapitulates phylogeny.

Babylon and the New Jerusalem are the apocalyptic cities which recapitulate history from opposing ends. It is true that they are symbols, but insofar as they reveal how humankind comes to be what it is, the substitution of either of these two cities for any other in the world is not to be done on a mechanical or arbitrary basis. It is all too easy to substitute Rome for Babylon, for example, and leave it go at that. But Rome is not needed for us to understand Babylon; just the opposite is the case. Likewise, Jerusalem is not needed for us to understand the New Jerusalem, but the contrary. Babylon is the reality and Rome the appearance; the New Jerusalem the reality and Jerusalem the appearance. What makes Babylon real is its origin in the city of Babel: humankind's archetypal attempt to create a world which stands over against God's. What makes the New Jerusalem real is its fulfillment of God's promise, hinted at in the selection of Jerusalem to be God's dwelling place among his people.

Jacques Ellul provides a summary note to this brief introductory treatment of the city: "The myth of the heavenly city appears as an appeal to transcend the works of man, that work in which he finds his peace and his haven. Thus the golden age will be characterized by an acceptance of history, and not by its refusal."[7]

This note also provides a bridge to a discussion of the city in science fiction—particularly as it reflects Babylon or the New Jerusalem. What becomes evident immediately is that the usual practice of linking the New Jerusalem with the utopian city (in the classical sense of that word) is, in light of what has thus far been discussed, an unfortunate practice. For utopian science fiction is premised on the refusal of history. In transferring utopia from isolation in space to isolation in time, *nowhere* becomes *nowhen*; the ideal city, the usual configuration of utopia, is cut off from history. Perhaps the most glaring example of this is to be found in B.F. Skinner's *Walden Two*, with its open disdain for history. "History is honored in Walden Two only as entertainment,"[8] says the host, Frazier, to his guests. And later, while discussing the educational system of the utopian community, Frazier comments: "We don't regard it [history] as essential in their education .... Nothing confuses our evaluation of the present more than a sense of history .... None of your myths, none of your heroes—no history, no destiny—simply the *Now*! The present is the thing. It's the only thing we can deal with anyway, in a scientific manner."[9] It is no surprise, then, that Walden Two itself has no real history (it appears as some see the New Jerusalem appearing, from beyond history); and, if Frazier has his way, it will never have one. "The founding of Walden Two is never recalled publicly by anyone who took part in it .... All personal contributions are either suppressed altogether or made anonymous. A simple historical log of the community is kept by the Legal Manager, but it is not consulted by anyone except Planners and Managers who need information."[10]

Similar presuppositions underlie many, if not most, utopian visions: they are refusals of history, in that they present a future city, but do not reveal to us how that city came to be—other than a wish fantasy, or a nightmare fantasy. The study of such fantasies may indeed be beneficial; however, our concern here is not to exalt the image of the city as apocalyptic over the city as utopian, but merely to systematically distinguish the two. How the two may be brought together is suggested by the following passage from Lewis Mumford:

> The prime need of the city today is for an intensification of collective self-knowledge, a deeper insight into the processes of history, as the first step toward discipline and control: such knowledge as is achieved by a neurotic patient in facing a long-buried infantile trauma that has stood in the way of his normal growth and integration.[11]

Disregard for history is not the case with the city in the Apocalypse of John. Although Babylon does stand for Rome, we are never allowed to forget that we cannot understand Rome unless we understand the history of Babylon, which is Babel. Similarly with the New Jerusalem: the vision of its descent is symbolically an acceptance of its history, not a refusal. For history is accepted in its fulfillment, which is announced from the beginning and becomes an integral part of the story.

When we attempt to come to grips with the city in our own time, we run into the same phenomenon: the refusal of history. In this vein Sam Bass Warner can write: "I have made the discovery that Americans have no urban history. They live in one of the world's most urbanized countries as though it were a wilderness in both time and space ... not conscious that they have a past and that by their actions they participate in making a future."[12] Grady Clay comes to nearly the same conclusion: "Early in this search [how to read the American city] I realized how little most Americans can find out about the evolution of their own ordinary surroundings."[13] Lewis Auchincloss, in speaking of New York City, particularizes these general statements: "The horror of living in New York is living in a city without a history."[14] And Anselm Strauss says of Detroit, "it appears to scorn its history."[15]

In short, the "Eternal Now" which characterized the ancient city has become the endless present: things have always been this way.

City planners, when they are thus cut off from the city's story, continue their search for the ever-elusive ideal city, utopia, the city as spatial artifact, resulting too often only in replacing an endless present with another—more pleasing to the eye, but just as deadly to the soul. Urban renewal becomes, in literary language, the attempt to produce an expurgated edition of the ancient city. To eliminate the slum from the spatial configuration of the city may be a worthwhile esthetic (and surely moral) goal; but history never forgets that the slum is "not simply . . . something to be wiped out in the name of hygiene . . . but a living part of a living city, with an intelligible past and future which must be rendered intelligible in relation to the whole."[16]

The treatment of the city in the Apocalypse of John is characterized by an acceptance of its history, not by a refusal. Babylon does stand for Rome, but it is Babylon which must be understood. In particular, it is Babylon as originating in Babel which tells us more about Rome than any exhaustive sociological, economic, or political analysis of the eternal city. To briefly review: Cain begets a son and builds a city. He gives the name Enoch to both, signifying that he seeks immortality through the city as well as through the son. Cain's descendants become "ancestors of all metal workers" (Gen. 4:22), signifying, as E.A. Speiser argues, that the "Cainite line is singled out here as the vehicle for mankind's technological progress."[17] The story of Cain, culminating in the episode of the building of the city of Babel and its tower, describes the solidification of "pride" in the form of a city: "Come, let us build ourselves a town and a tower with its top reaching heaven. Let us make a name for ourselves, so that we may not be scattered about the whole earth" (Gen. 11:4).

In all the various descriptions of the city in Genesis 4-11, the city stands as the attempt by humankind to create its own source of power, to give an order to life, to provide security and fulfillment, to create a paradise which was lost. Always the city stands in opposition to God, because it invites humankind to place its trust in the efforts of princes rather than in the promises of God. To vastly oversimplify: Genesis 4-11 is a sociological analysis of sin, equal in weight and import to Genesis 1-3, which is the psychological analysis. The basic flaw is the same: pride. But the pride in Genesis 4-11 is the pride of a city-nation and its technology.

A reading of the Apocalypse of John recapitulates the history of the city as given in the Bible, revealing in effect that Rome is Babel/Babylon reborn. Rome must fall in the final analysis not because it is evil and corrupt (through its persecution of the Christian community), but primarily because it is Babylon. For John, Rome is not the city of someone else's history, wreaking havoc on the Christian community; Rome is the city of his own people's history. What is being purged and purified is not just a city; it is the history of pride and self-assertion. The invitation is to repent; not to flee an evil place, but to leave behind a sinful life.

The fall of Babylon, furthermore, is the end of this world, literally, at least according to one literary tradition which is incorporated in the Apocalypse of John. For immediately after its fall, songs of victory are sung in the heavens (Rev. 19:1-4). The city in this tradition is revealed not as the last stronghold of man against his fellow man, but as the last stronghold of humankind against God. Sin is never doing the "new thing" it always appears to be; it is always the same old sin, from beginning to end, pride. It is God who makes all things new.

The fall of Babylon, finally, is noteworthy in that it transpires in so short a time:

> Mourn, mourn for this great city
> Babylon, so powerful a city,
> doomed as you are within a single hour. (Rev. 18:10)

Dylan's apocalypse, in "Talkin' World War Three Blues," lasted only fifteen minutes. The majority of doomsday stories in science fiction likewise treat of the end in a very perfunctory manner. What can this mean except to underline the fact that the works of man are very precarious, their continued existence hangs on the thinnest of threads? Catastrophe is all the more terrifying for its suddenness, the almost instantaneous revelation of the utter emptiness and hollowness of this supposedly indestructible artifact built up for centuries: both the metal, glass and plastic artifact, and the artifact of political power and its shadow governments. The ultimate revelation of Babylon's sudden collapse and fall is that perhaps there is nothing there after all!

Science fiction is often characterized as being apocalyptic; and so it is. But not merely in the commonly understood sense of that term, as being a warning of doom and destruction, a death-wish fantasy escape from the harsh realities of the present. There is that tone in much of science fiction, to be sure; just as it is there in much inter-testamental and early Christian apocalyptic. But others of it is apocalyptic in the fuller sense of being a revelation of the future as a dimension of the present, a literature which wrestles with promise, fulfillment and future insofar as they stand in critical relationship to the present, a literature which speaks of judgment and renewal in the most uncompromising terms. The judgment is always a judgment of the present. These topics will be taken up more fully in subsequent chapters. It remains now to discuss briefly some of the literary devices used in science fiction to speak of the city as a temporal image. These raise the issue of the unfolding of history; and the unfolding of history is central to all apocalyptic, biblical and secular.

From what has been discussed so far, it is obvious that utopia does not function as a vehicle of recapitulation. Utopia is fundamentally a-historical. It may very well provide some useful images of what lies ahead for the city, but it does not reveal the historical dimension of our being. Utopia is not a story, it is a plan; it presents the city as a spatial image. If we push this image to its limits in the literature of science fiction, as Henri Gougaud does in his book on the demons and marvels of science fiction, the city becomes symbolic of the desire to close in on the self, to return to the womb. The spatial structure of the future city itself speaks of this desire: the domed city is a womb in which humankind is nourished and protected against the onslaughts of change and the terrors of history.[18] There are numerous references in the current literature to the enclosed shopping malls, and more frequently to the walled security subdivisions (notice their utopian names: Paradise Estates, Camelot, Chevy Chase, etc.) harking back to the feudal ages of castles and moats. The domed city takes us back even further, past history into myth: the sky becomes again a bowl. The original question, formulated early on in the awakening of human consciousness, comes back to haunt us: Do the gods have any real need for humankind? It is not asked this bluntly, of course. In the symbolic language of the domed city, to translate it into present thought categories, it is suggested that "utopia" operates perfectly without people—in fact better. People may live in utopia, but they must function as servo-mechanisms, as automata and robots. There can be no vital interaction with the world outside, for this would invite change, a disruption of the system, and chaos would result.

Alas! People have always frustrated the best laid plans. They refuse to live according to someone else's blueprints. Thus, while utopia endures as ideal plan, it fails miserably as story—for it has no end. Neither is it possible to make utopia a livable, inhabitable place. The dull stories of utopian societies, in which "nothing happens," mirror perfectly the dull society itself in which nothing happens. Utopia is no help in revealing historical consciousness. Only the end will do that. Yet, in science fiction, there are devices employed which seek to explore temporal consciousness and our awareness of how things come to be. Before talking about the end (doomsday), it may be useful to look briefly at three of these devices: time travel, parallel worlds and future history.

Although the device of time travel is capable of many different interpretations, it can be read as a method of talking about the city as an historical entity. In this most benign of all possible interpretations, time travel literally places all of time and history before the reader in a living relationship. It makes time and history present in a developmental process. The past is never really over and done with; it is still somehow present to us. The future likewise is never totally out in front of us; it is contained seminally in the present, and can break into the present at any moment.

What is striking in science fiction is that time travel is accomplished today less and less through the medium of a machine, and more and more through the development of psychic and para-psychological powers. The import of the trend, it seems to me, is the recognition that time is not only a physical dimension but is also a psychological one. Past and future are psychological dimensions to the present, which must be explored if we are truly to appreciate the critical importance of the present. This is particularly true in reference to the topic under discussion, the city. The "future city" is not somewhere or somewhen else; it is the city as it is revealed in our hope. Likewise the ancient city is the city as it is revealed in our memory. Hope and memory have always been the premier means of time travel. But *what* is revealed in memory and hope is not so important for our concern as the *how*: the fact that there is symbolized in time travel the belief that one can get there from here.

There is another device in science fiction even more compelling than that of time travel: the parallel world. Like time travel it, too, is undergoing a change, away from the parallel world of space, to the parallel world of time, history, and probability. The parallel world is no longer a simple extrapolation of present trends into the future; it is rather a radically new perspective on the present's relationship to the past and to the future. The creation of a parallel world of probability shakes our confidence in the solid ground of the real and the present. In this device we encounter the apocalyptic in science fiction. The parallel world drives us to a radical confrontation with our most cherished belief: that we know the difference between appearance and reality, especially insofar as we view appearance and reality as temporal manifestations.

Critics talk of the estrangement which results when we view an object from a new perspective, an estrangement which fosters cognition. This is precisely what is happening in the creation of a parallel world of probability. But the resulting cognition leads to our being able to imagine new processes, not merely to our understanding new configurations. If the smallest shift in remote time can create such different probability worlds (see Ray Bradbury's "A Sound of Thunder," where stepping on a plant in prehistoric times results in a shift from contemporary democratic to totalitarian government), then present decisions entail consequences with which to be reckoned. In short, the parallel world is a reminder that we are held accountable for the way things are—if only in terms of how we write our histories, past and future.

This brings us to our final consideration: the future history preoccupation of science fiction. It is here that the critical correlation of science fiction and apocalypse finds its most fertile ground. For just as there is a consensus history shared by the inter-testamental and early Christian apocalyptic, so there is a consensus future history present in science fiction. Major sources of this future history include Asimov's *Foundation Trilogy*, Heinlein's *The Past through Tomorrow: Future History Stories* and James Blish's *Cities in Flight*.

The temptation is to read these stories as projections into the future; but there is ample evidence throughout that they are stories of the past as well. Here is the crux: The writing of history is never done with. For the past is as much a world of probability as is the future. The deliberate shifting of the time of composition in apocalyptic signals the same intent: we are responsible for the past insofar as we write its history.

The issue brought to a head by these three devices in science fiction is this: the city's existence is as precarious as our understanding of it. To put it another way: the city is built with words as well as with blueprints. If we understand this city only in spatial terms, it may well last forever, but not so its inhabitants. In temporal terms, however, the city always engages us to become more radically aware of our historicity—and both the city and we change in the process. Thus the stories we tell about the city reveal the consciousness we have of historical change.

James Blish's *Cities in Flight*, a marvelous treasurehouse of symbols, is a case in point. Here the cities, by means of a device called a "spin-dizzy," tear themselves up by their roots, flee from the dying suburbs, and travel as self-contained units through the wilderness of space and time. On a cosmic scale all history is cyclic: time as well as space is curved. (Blish models his history on Spengler's cycles.) But the focal point of Blish's cycle, if not the hub, is the present—as the very message of the narrative tells us. Thus Blish's tale tells of the past and the future as they are realized in the present through their retelling. The story is a universe, too; and at the center of the story is the city—as has always been the case.

When we look at the stories told about the city in science fiction today, we find that it does not tell tales so much about Babylon and the New Jerusalem as it does about New York and Los Angeles. To contrast the future histories of these two cities as they are depicted in science fiction is illuminating, for it highlights the differences which exist between the city as spatial and the city as temporal artifact, between the city as utopian and the city as apocalyptic.

New York always remains New York. Although variously described in its future history as a battleground, a relic, or a museum, it always stands only for itself. Los Angeles, on the other hand, becomes Disneyland, Hollywood, and nameless urban sprawl. It invariably stands for anything but itself. Thomas Pynchon's description of San Narciso in *The Crying of Lot 49* sums up what can and has been said about it: "Like many named places in California it was less an identifiable city than a grouping of concepts—census tracts, special purpose bond-issue districts, shopping nuclei, all overlaid with access roads to its own freeway.[19]

New York recapitulates the history of the city; Los Angeles seeks to be that wholly new creation of humankind, which is precisely its ultimate doom. Now, all cities stand under the judgment of doom, from Babel to Los Angeles. But the doom which faces the proto-typical Los Angeles, being the spatial image of the city, is all the more terrifying in that Los Angeles is not able to understand its fullness to come, for it is lacking the dimension of past and future. Ignorant of its birth and growth, it dies still not comprehending. Babel, on the other hand, and all its descendants (from Babylon to Rome to

Washington) live in the knowledge of their birth and death, however vague the comprehension.

There are more than enough indications in science fiction that its writers are aware of the cities' lineage, again however vague the comprehension. The cities of science fiction by and large are the proud descendants of Cain, technological marvels of plastic, glass and steel. The genetics of pride, tied as it is to technology and the city in Genesis 4-11, gives birth to the city as machine—literally, in some stories. Two anthologies in particular document the future of the city in this age of genetic experimentation: *Cities of Wonder*, edited by Damon Knight, which includes the classics "By the Waters of Babylon," by Stephen Vincent Benet, and "The Machine Stops," by E.M. Forster; and *Future City*, edited by Roger Elwood. In the latter, I might add, there does not appear one account of the city as utopia. The following is just a sample of themes running through its stories: New York city is open for sight-seeing tours only during the summer months; people trapped inside completely mechanized buildings die when the power fails; freeways become battle grounds; homosexuality becomes necessary as a survival technique in an over-populated world; apartment hunting becomes that literally: those who refuse to vacate at age 65 are hunted and killed; city doctors treat city sicknesses, and "kill" the city if it is incurable; Chicago runs so smoothly when no one is present that the computers prevent people from entering; traffic officers routinely execute violators as a means of controlling the population. As Vonnegut would say: So it goes!

In an afterword to Elwood's collection, Frederick Pohl concludes that the city's survival in the face of all the indictments leveled against it is the "paradox that guarantees the future of the city as an institution."[20] This paradox is none other than the groping acceptance of the city's ancestry in Cain and its future in the New Jerusalem, that is, the realization that the city is both utopian and apocalyptic. We have chosen to highlight the apocalypse because it tends to be slighted in the literature about the ideal city. Thus we conclude that in speaking of the future city in the terms noted above, the writers of science fiction have begun to understand the city's past and its future; in short, its existence in history. In doing so, they have much to contribute to the creation of truly liberating communities. Our presupposition throughout has been that we are city people. Our history, in the Bible, begins and ends with the city—from the city of Cain to the city of the New Jerusalem. What is begun by humankind is taken up and transformed by God. But it is not only space that is taken up, it is also time and history. To turn our backs and flee from the city on our initiative is to flee from ourselves, to refuse to remain open to the transforming and saving acts of God.

History is known in its fulfillment, as well as in its beginnings. And thus far only one city has understood its own history in its fullness—Jerusalem, as it is revealed to us in the New Jerusalem. To paraphrase Paul: "It knows as it has been known." In the New Jerusalem we possess recapitulatively another version of the Bible's one movement, but this time according to a sociological perspective. For in the New Jerusalem God once again takes on the "human condition," the city becomes symbolically God's incarnate presence among humankind: "I saw that there was no temple in the city since the Lord God Almighty and the Lamb were themselves the temple, and the city did not need the sun or the moon for light, since it was lit by the radiant glory of God" (Rev. 21:22-23).

At length we come to the end: Doomsday. And doomsday, strangely enough, is where it all comes together, not where it all falls apart. The resolution becomes the re-solution: the method by which new relationships are seen. The riddles of life and history are not solved; rather their mystery is seen as such for the first time.

Let me begin by reviewing some material already covered, in order to get a perspective on where doomsday fits into the scheme of things. At the beginning we talked about the nature of apocalyptic literature and the function it plays: to give people hope—in history, in the contemporaneity of life, and in its continuity. Robert Jay Lifton identified the need apocalyptic fills as a "compelling and universal urge to maintain a sense of immortality in the face of biological death. Life," he continues, "requires a perception of the connection extending beyond that annihilation ... a language to express this sense of biohistorical continuity." In Christian apocalyptic terms this is the struggle which ends in the triumph of life *out of* death, as opposed to life *after* death. For life after death negates the meaning and purpose of apocalypse. It undermines the historicity of the struggle and the value of resistance. It places the resolution outside history, and thus denies the central given of biblical faith: God acts through history and reveals himself in history. Life out of death, on the other hand, situates the meaning, purpose and fulfillment of life within history; these are to be found in the daily struggle to bring creation to completion.

Apocalyptic literature arises in response to a situation in which people are tempted to look for life after death, thereby avoiding the struggle necessary to bring life out of death. Apocalyptic is neither a literature of escape (the next world is all that matters), nor of revolution (this present world and its time is all that matters). It is a literature of the present. The present is important in apocalyptic literature because it contains seminally the future; or, in other terms, the present is that into which the future breaks suddenly and radically. There is, however, a dark optimism pervading apocalyptic literature. Things always get worse before they get better. Still, apocalyptic invites us to be open to the presence of all time in the present, to discover the seeds, the embryo of life existing here and now, and to await creatively the coming of the radically new. For it is this living relationship to the present works of God which is the reference point for immortality, the biohistorical continuity of life in the face of biological death.

At the core of apocalyptic, then, there stands the problem of time and history, of this life and the next, of the past, the present and the future. We have seen how technology seeks to obliterate the sense of time through the myth of the inevitability of progress. We have also seen how the city as the supreme technological work of humankind can destroy our relationship both to time and to nature, how thus conceived it portrays both nature and time as the enemies of humankind, to be conquered and destroyed.

But let us go back even further. Our reflections have at various times touched on the bomb and its presence in our lives. The bomb causes a rupture in the fabric of life, creating an immediacy and an inevitability which tends to destroy any sense of the meaning and purpose of life. We cited Jefferson Airplane and Dylan, among others, who chronicled the sickness caused by the threat of nuclear war, still the most striking image of doomsday we have—and, need it be noted, once again casting its shadow over life.

The bomb severs us from our sense of time because, on the one hand (insofar as it is inevitable) it forces us to put all our eggs in the basket of the immediate future. Thus the girl in Dylan's "Talkin' World War III Blues," who refuses his request to play "Adam and Eve," is not able to start building for the future in the only place where it can be done—in the present. On the other hand, the bomb disrupts our sense of time (insofar as it creates an immediacy) by consuming all the people's energies. Physically it is doing this in the ballooning military budgets worldwide; but psychologically it consumes ever more. It cuts people off from the past (all the past has ever done is give the bomb to us) and the future (all the future will do is deliver us to the bomb). The only time left is the present—and there is nowhere to go with it!

In *A Case of Conscience*, James Blish describes this inhuman condition with apocalyptic insight. Ruiz-Sanchez, a Jesuit priest, reflects on what the nuclear arms race is doing to people. He recalls the beginnings, first of the arms race and now of the shelter race:

The shelter race had been undertaken under the dawning realization that the threat of nuclear war is not only imminent but transcendent. . . .

In response to the objection that humankind has always lived "on the verge," Ruiz-Sanchez replies:

But no, it's quite different now. The pestilence was capricious: one's children might survive it; but fusion bombs are catholic." He winced involuntarily. "And there it is. A moment ago I caught myself thinking that the shadow of destruction we labor under now is not only imminent but transcendent; I was burlesquing a tragedy; death in premedical days was always both imminent and immanent, impending and indwelling—but it was never transcendent. In those days, only God was impending, indwelling, *and* transcendent all at once, and that was their hope. Today, we've given them death instead.[21]

The insight of Ruiz-Sanchez is profound: after death the only thing left will be death. This is what it means for death to become transcendent. The point made by Ruiz-Sanchez about those days cannot be stressed too strongly; God alone is immanent (dwelling within the being of the world) and transcendent (existing beyond the being of the world). For God it is not a matter of either/or; it is both/and. Such is the nature of God. But the bomb has threatened even this! For nuclear detente (the constant threat of impending war) has created the situation in which death is seen as both immanent and transcendent. This situation happens because of the causal implications of the before/after perspective, especially when it continually insists on speaking of "life after death."

When people's lives are shaped by what might happen at any moment, then there is a sense in which it can be said that "what might happen at any moment" causes the future. When everything depends on what is impending, what is impending might be said to be the cause, not only of what will be, but also and more importantly of what is. And if death alone is seen as "what might happen," death is seen lurking in every moment of existence, waiting behind every button. It becomes immanent. The final step is quite easily taken; suddenly death exists everywhere, even after death. Death becomes transcendent, the only reality left to endure after the great holocaust, after doomsday.[22]

It is in terms of immanence and transcendence, then, that our first consideration of doomsday takes form. For what people imagine *beyond* doomsday reveals what they imagine *within* it. It should be pointed out that this consideration abstracts from the ordinary notions and perceptions of time as a linear phenomenon; or rather, it sublates them; it uses them by going beyond them. We are not talking here about a *before* and an *after*, but a beyond and within. A before and an after, considered simply linearly, leads all too easily to the appreciation of the transcendence of nuclear death alone, without its immanence.

There is something to be said about doomsday in itself, and not merely as an incident on a line stretching somewhere from the past to somewhere in the future. What exists beyond the nuclear doomsday exists now within it. (This is not the same, however, if we speak of "after" doomsday.) In the perspective of "beyond" doomsday, doomsday itself symbolizes the birth pangs of the new creation; the deliverance, not the end. Doomsday is the way in which all of life and history and time is transformed, not the way in which it is destroyed. It is the way in which all of life is seen as continuous, not ruptured. Doomsday is the re-affirmation that life comes out of death, not after death.

When time is seen only as a linear phenomenon, as a progression from one point to another, then the result is that doomsday becomes the utter destruction of all reality. Doomsday becomes necessary in such a conceptual framework as the device to get from one point to another alone the same line. Thus, among the most famous and oft-repeated lines in science fiction are these: "After the great war," "After the Third World War," "Ninety years after the terrible nuclear holocaust," and so forth. Doomsday happens at the drop of a hat in apocalyptic science fiction. But science fiction is not alone in this.

This is much the same problem which confronted the early church; for it had to contend with the issue of the impending Second Coming. What was happening to the early Christians (concerned only with the impending return of Jesus and the subsequent deliverance from the evils of the world) was similar in many ways to what is now happening to humankind living on the edge of doom. But the temptation, then as now, was to view history and life only in terms of before and after, forgetting the beyond which is also the within.

The Apocalypse of John, in order to counteract such prevailing sensibilities, situates the Christian community as living not at the edge of doom, or at the brink of doom, but rather *within* doom— literally, in the middle of doomsday. In the Apocalypse of John, doomsday, for all practical purposes, is anti-climactic. It could hardly be otherwise, after the plagues, wars, famines, pestilence, persecutions and purges which have swept the world in those few short chapters. This may also be the reason for the casualness with which science fiction writers often treat of doomsday. It is indeed difficult in the Apocalypse of John to nail down exactly where and when doomsday happens. Scholars have isolated at least two different literary traditions fused together in the text. Each of these traditions, moreover, contains at least two descriptions of doomsday. One centers around the fall of Babylon; the other around the great eschatological war, the final battle between God and the Beast who leads the forces of evil. These are found in the following places:

	Tradition "A"	Tradition "B"
Fall of Babylon	18: 1-3	18: 4-8
Final War	20: 7-10	19: 11-21

In addition, we must also consider the description of doomsday found in the story of Armageddon, the name place most often associated with doomsday. The text is Rev.16: 12-16. Finally, there is the description of the final judgment, which also reflects the doomsday theme. Here again each tradition provides its description: "A" 20: 13-15; "B" 20: 11-12.

In the Apocalypse of John, then, doomsday happens so often that one is almost forced to conclude that doomsday is no more than a way of looking at the present. Doomsday is apocalyptic precisely because it is a revelation of what is happening now, not what will be happening in the future, immediate or distant. That future will be no worse or better than the present; for the future is contained seminally in the present. At the same time, however, things will always get worse before they get better—because this is what characterizes the trauma of birth. There is no reason to fear the future any more than the present, nor is there any reason to trust it more than the present—for the future is contained seminally in the present. That is, the future is critically present; the future reveals more of the present than the present reveals of itself. In short, it reveals the openness of the present to the radically new. What it asks is simply to be open in the present to the coming of the radically new in the only way the radically new can come: through the trauma of birth. What characterizes birth is neither a blinding fear of the unknown nor a blinding trust in the unknown, but rather a hope in the potential of life. Life does not come after birth, it comes through birth. Life is not beyond birth, it is within.

But let us pursue the doomsday theme from another angle. Doomsday, it is said, reflects the hostility of many science fiction writers, their paranoia (as Ketterer suggests), or their disillusionment (as I have argued). Yet one would have difficulty in citing passages, books or images which surpass the dark optimism pervading the Apocalypse of John. The key, of course, is in the phrase "dark optimism," and in how it functions in relation to the tension between immanence and transcendence. When that tension is seen merely as a relationship between before and after, then what comes after negates what has gone before. The passage undergone is simply and only a passage from worse to better. The after is simply and only a judgment on the before. John, on the other hand, constantly reminds us that things always get worse before they get better. There can be no simple, linear, temporal judgment on the effectiveness of passage through doomsday. Doomsday of itself is no unequivocal statement that the old has passed away and the new has come into existence. It may be that the new has also passed away—that is a possibility always to be considered. And, indeed, as history reminds us, this is often the case.

Viewed from the perspective of the beyond and within, however, the focus shifts. In this perspective to move beyond is also to move within. In addition, the beyond/within sublates the before/after. Thus, to see what comes after is also to see more clearly what has gone before. Doomsday, thus, is a critical understanding of the present—the openness of the present to the possibility that there is nothing here after all! This, I maintain, most appropriately understood is the disillusionment contained in much science fiction. Disillusionment much more than hostility or paranoia, is closer to the dark optimism of John in his Apocalypse. For disillusionment forces people to look more deeply into the within of things. Elsewhere I will discuss at greater length the critical function of the future, particularly as reflected in linear extrapolative and post-catastrophe science fiction stories. It is here where the initial observations can be made. Neither Ben Bova's *Millenium* nor Pier Anthony's *Battle Circle* explores the present disillusionment seriously enough to allow a deeper understanding of and insight into what is really going on in the present. Thus *Millenium* edges closer and closer to paranoia in the final judgment it makes on the present state of affairs—there are forces at work presently which seek to destroy the rational, logical, scientific understanding and ordering of the world. And *Battle Circle* displays a nearly undisguised contempt for what exists at the present, seeking salvation completely in the future. Neither sees within and into the present, because they cannot see beyond it. They merely see after. What is revealed finally is that there is nothing here in the present after all! The present is empty, without hope, without future.

The dark optimism of John counters the easy satisfying answers of hostility and paranoia with a deepening of the disillusionment: things always get worse before they get better. There is no one, final doomsday after all; doomsday is woven into the very fabric of life. One must pass through doomsday to get to the other side. Doomsday is apocalyptic because it is a revelation of what is on the other side, of what is beyond but not merely after. In fact, doomsday is so central to apocalyptic literature and imagination that apocalypse is almost synonymous with doomsday. But it must be understood in the radical sense to be fully appreciated. Doomsday reveals what it all comes down to in the end.

There is a distinction to be made at this point, between *passing through* and *getting past* doomsday. Much science fiction is "uncanonical" in the same way much inter-testamental apocalyptic is: it is concerned primarily with getting past doomsday. The only revelation to come in such narratives of doomsday is that the author has failed to see doomsday taking place here and now. In terms used above, the author has failed to see doomsday contained seminally in the present, and failed to see that, indeed, it is breaking into the present. When doomsday is seen as merely impending, about to happen in the immediate or distant future, then the only tempting tactic is to get past it with the least effort or involvement. Doomsday in such a conceptual framework becomes merely another obstacle. In the Bible, on the other hand, doomsday is a revelation. But it is even more; doomsday, in some strange sense, is fulfillment—and even more still, doomsday is consummation.

To speak of fulfillment and consummation leads us to the second part of our discussion of doomsday, and the real meaning it possesses: judgment. Reference was made above to this dimension of doomsday, when we discussed the different literary traditions contained in the Apocalypse of John. Let me cite one of the passages in full:

> Then I saw a great white throne and the one who was sitting on it. In his presence, earth and sky vanished, leaving no trace. I saw the dead, both great and small, standing in front of his throne, while the book of life was opened, and other books opened which were the record of what they had done in their lives, by which the dead were judged.
>
> The sea gave up all the dead who were in it; Death and Hades were emptied of the dead who were in them; and everyone was judged according to the way in which he had lived. Then Death and Hades were thrown into the burning lake. This burning lake is the second death; and anybody whose name could not be found written in the book of life was thrown into the burning lake. (Rev. 20: 11-15)

It is only at this point that the finality of doomsday begins to sink in. Beyond doomsday, in this episode, has all the characteristics of after doomsday. Judgment in the biblical world is almost the point of no return, a cut off so decisive, so final that it calls for a disruption, something so drastic as a "second death." Romano Guardini, in his commentary on the Apocalypse of John, describes it in the following terms:

> This is judgment. It is the probing, testing point of the judge's blade into all being. The apocalyptic offensive of the eternal . . . against transitory history, a *coup* that convulses the world. It lifts her off the hinges of her security, out of the placidness of her existence, so completely that heaven and earth "flee" . . . .

Further on Guardini continues:

> Judgment, the fulfiller of existence, is infallible. Appearances are torn down. Imitation, irrelevance crumble away. Truth alone remains. Man becomes precisely that which eternal mercy and his own will have made him.

The remotest, finest consequences are drawn. The individual becomes completely himself, fashioned entirely of his own deeds, his own attitude. The ultimate unifying of his being takes place—here, before the throne. In this unprotected encounter with God, man receives himself; completely, finally. While on earth, where he had only himself, he could deceive that self, fly from self. Here though he is himself undivided and unconcealed. He no longer yearns for his own truths, he no longer needs to collect or unravel the loose ends of his being. Through God he has become the exact product of his earthly existence, without a single shadow of obscurity. And so he remains throughout eternity, though it is false to use the word remains here, which would be speaking in time; so he simply *is*.[23]

I will take up a little later the topic of God's final judgment, especially Guardini's contention that God's judgment is infallible. More pertinent to our discussion at this point is the statement that judgment is the "fulfillment" of existence; that is, judgment fulfills existence. It is this facet of doomsday which is most critical in our analysis of the doomsday theme in the stories of science fiction. For the future world stands before the judgment seat of science fiction writers in their descriptions of doomsday after doomsday lying in wait along the paths the world now walks unawares.

No one should be taken aback by the finality of their judgments; for implicit in judgment is finality. Doomsday is terrible, not because it is final (we have seen that in the first part of our discussion), but because it carries with it the element of judgment, a judgment, moreover, striking to the core of existence, separating the good from the evil.

What the writers of science fiction are doing, therefore, is pronouncing their judgment on the world. And the device they most often use is the nuclear doomsday. In this they are remarkably close to the methodology and style of the Apocalypse of John. But although there is this note of finality to doomsday as judgment, still doomsday is not the end. In the Apocalypse of John, judgment is critical to the emergence of the new heaven and the new earth. It is almost as though the new creation springs out of the judgment of the old; or, as we have been contending all along, life comes out of death. At any rate, there is some kind of cathartic effect to judgment being pronounced on the world. For then one is able, in turn, to await in a new way the emergence of the new world, of life out of death.

Science fiction rarely discourses directly on judgment being the fulfiller of existence. But it pursues the topic obliquely. There has always been in science fiction a preoccupation with history and the rewriting of history. In this sense science fiction explores the topic of history as the fulfiller of existence. Indeed, one could conceivably rephrase the dictum of Guardini to read: "History fulfills existence." For it is not only the future world which stands before the judgment seat of science fiction; the past world stands there also. Technological imagination provides the revisionist science fiction "historians" with something remarkably similar to angel's guided tours or God-inspired dreams: a look at the past, usually through time travel or the time machine. This look is often as frightening and as intriguing as a look at the future. There is an ambiguity to many of these endeavors. In *Childhood's End*, Arthur C. Clark describes as well as anyone what might be the result of actually having access to the past "as it really was":

> Though it had always been obvious to any rational mind that *all* the world's religious writings could not be true, the shock was nevertheless profound. Here was a revelation which no one could doubt or deny; here, seen by some unknown magic of Overlord science, were the true beginnings of all the world's great faiths .... All the good and all the evil they had wrought were swept suddenly into the past, and could touch the minds of men no more.[24]

Clarke goes on to describe, in the novel, the subsequent decline of science, too. (Though this should hardly surprise, given the distorted appreciation of science witnessed to in the passage quoted above. The device cannot be doubted or denied; it was some unknown "magic." This is hardly a basis for science!)

Childhood's End is content with describing what would happen if one were to view history as it really happened. It is Philip H. Dick, however, who most constantly engages in the tactic of rewriting history, past, present and future. *The Man in the High Castle* contains two examples of this process. The mainline narrative describes a world in which the Axis powers (Germany, Italy and Japan) have defeated the Allies during World War II. In the course of the narrative, the history of WWII, along with the contemporary present history, is constantly being rewritten. But two further swipes at history and its rewriting are taken; for the book contains excerpts from and continual reference to another book, written by "the man in the high castle." This second book, in turn, describes a world in which the Allies have defeated the Axis powers. Neither of the two worlds, however, the revised version of the outcome of WWII nor the fictional account of our present world, is anywhere near similar to the world we are familiar with. But they could be! This is what the book is about. The book argues that this world, described twice, although differently each time, is exactly the world we know and are familiar with. Indeed, it is the only world we know: the world of chance, luck, fate.

Central to understanding the novel are the references to and use of the *I Ching* or *The Book of Changes*. The characters are constantly consulting the sticks and ideograms. The book within the book, "The Grasshopper Lies Heavy," it is revealed, was written with the help of an oracle. The author's wife explains: "One by one Hawth made the choices. Thousands of them. By means of the lines. Historic period. Subject. Character. Plot."[25] When the author himself is pushed by his wife to ask the oracle why it wrote the book it did, the oracle replies, "Inner truth." But Hawthorne cannot be forced to conclude that his book is the truth, that Germany and Japan did in fact lose the war. And so comes the final crisis—evaluating the truth of written history, when both what "actually happened" and what is written are based on luck, fate and chance.

"Even you didn't face it," Juliana said. For a time he considered. His gaze had become empty, Juliana saw. Turned inward, she realized. Preoccupied by himself . . . and then his eyes became clear again; he grunted, started.
"I'm not sure of anything," he said.
"Believe," Juliana said.
He shook his head no.[26]

Hawthorne was asked to interpret the truth of historical events, when, in fact, he had seen the task to be one of interpreting fate, luck and chance. The latter is the subject matter of historians.

One may construe this to be a cynical view of history and its writing with which *The Man in the High Castle* concludes. But per se it needs be so for all who (re)-write history; whether they do it by consulting the *I Ching* or sitting in the comfort of their academic surroundings. There is so much which does rely on chance, in history itself and in the writing of history. It is difficult to sort out what affects the subsequent course of history more, the facts or the history of those facts. The operative saying, in this vein of thought, is, History will be the judge. What is usually meant, however, is that historians will be the judge. And the goal is to make sure that it is one's own historians who survive or prevail to write the history.

As if to underline this cynicism, Dick explores the explicitly manipulative function of the "history of the winners" in *The Penultimate Truth*. The "war" has happened. But for the people who live underground in the "tanks" created during that war (and this comprises 90% of the population), the war is still in progress. Above ground the elite few are constantly rewriting the present and past to give credibility to the on-going war, waged between the Western Democracies (Wes-Dem) and the Eastern Communists. In reality it is all one government.

Once again various characters engage in rewriting the whole of World War II, in the form of documentaries used to indoctrinate the people. An example:

> It was the British who had brought about Buchenwald, was Gottlied Fishcher's revised history. Not the Germans. The Germans were the *victims*, in 1943 as much as in 1919. A later scene in Documentary A would show Berliners in 1944, hunting in the woods surrounding Berlin, searching for nettles to make into soup. The Germans were starving; all continental Europe, all people inside and outside concentration camps, were starving. Because of the British. . . .
>
> *Why run the thing?* . . . . The peculiarities of Hitler's personal character (after all, he had been subjected to great and prolonged stress during World War One and the Weimer Depression period, as had all Germans) had misled the rather phlegmatic Anglo-Saxon peoples into imagining that Hitler was "dangerous." Actually—and in episode after episode, Alex Sourberry would purr out this message—the Wes-Dem TV viewer would discover that England, France, Germany and the United States should all have been allies. Against the authentic evil-doer, Josef Stalin, with his megalomaniacal plans for world conquest . . . proved by the actions of the USSR in the post-war period—a period in which even Churchill had to admit that Soviet Russia *was* the enemy.[27]

The reason behind the reason, however, the elite few argue, is that the people in the tanks must be duped to remain there voluntarily, thereby allowing the radiation from the real war to dissipate. The question that emerges, and this is a question rarely asked, is this: who are the losers of the war?

Central to the task of much writing and rewriting of history is what could be called the "doomsday theory": the belief that it is not possible to get from one point in time to another without an intervening catastrophe. The catastrophe need not be the event of a final doomsday, as we have noted; for doomsday happens again and again; it is woven into the very fabric of life. It is this doomsday theory which allows history to be used in a manipulative manner; in much the same way that the impending threat of nuclear war (or death, or hell) is used to manipulate people. This is that Ruiz-Sanchez meant when he said that the threat had become transcendent; he meant that it had become necessary.And there is nothing like necessity to get people to do what they would not otherwise do.

Doomsday becomes, then, not only a way of reading the future; it also becomes a way of reading the past. All of history is seen as hanging on a few critical choices, and/or as being a reaction to some few critical catastrophes. The choices made, moreover, were "necessary"; they had to be made if the world was to survive. History in this sense fulfills existence only insofar as some few people want to judge the world in light of their own narrow vision. Such a history is always a history of the elite few, as *The Penultimate Truth* so perceptibly points out. It is by and large, unfortunately, the one history we are all too familiar with.

The same holds true for rewriting the history of the future. The future is now manipulated by the few through the tactic of nuclear detente. The future is taken away from people through the threat of the bomb (e.g., Blish), through consumer credit (e.g., Kornbluth and Pohl, in *The Space Merchants*), through government surveillance (e.g., Orwell, in *1984*), and/or through drugs, sense satisfaction and genetic engineering (e.g., Huxley, in *Brave New World*).

So much for the writing and rewriting of history—past, present and future. It is all written from the end, looking back. Even future history is a matter of looking back from an end, imagined as having taken place or having been achieved, and now providing a vantage point from which to survey the program being made.

Apocalypse judges history, its writing and rewriting, from a vantage point not human in making. Or so it claims. It is as difficult to believe this as it was for Hawthorne (in *The Man in the High Castle*) to believe that luck, fate, chance really determine the course of events and their interpretation. But an immanent and transcendent end to history is, it seems, a necessary corollary to an immanent and transcendent God. In fact, as will be argued later, belief in an imminent end is a necessary consequence of belief in a transcendent God. Be that as it may, a discussion of history as fulfiller and judge of existence cannot be resolved unless the vantage point of apocalyptic is granted. Far from taking away the future, apocalyptic offers us a future by taking away all the limited, closed, narrow futures boxing us in every which way we turn. Again, just as belief in God opens up (undergirds, reveals, transforms, whatever) new dimensions of human existence; so belief in an end (divinely grounded) opens up new dimensions of historical existence. Much more on this topic in subsequent chapters. For now we must conclude the present topic, judgment.

All judgments made in the rewriting of history are not infallible. But in its own way, history is. The final judgment of history (i.e., made upon, or by, history) is infallible. Thus we must take up the topic of judgment dropped so quickly before.

According to the apocalyptic insight, judgment is the consummation of existence, of all creation. In the Bible, the phrases "Day of judgment" and "Day of Consummation" are used almost interchangeably. We will note elsewhere that apocalyptic, with its insistence on the final, irrevocable, nature of God's judgment, acts as counter to the prophetic emphasis on the conditional nature of God's judgment. Indeed, apocalyptic argues for judgment through consummation, and for consummation through judgment. But it must always be noted that the judgment is God's, not humankind's. At some final point in time and in space there is limit, boundary, end. Many others have noted this and have explored the meanings.

I want now to take up the theme of judgment as it operates in apocalyptic as a recapitulation. Apocalypse itself recapitulates the whole of the Bible. Again a common theme of commentators. The Apocalypse of John symbolically ties the whole Bible together— from the beginning to the end—by speaking of the great serpent (the snake in Genesis) and the river (the setting for Eden) and the tree. But within these symbols there lies also deeper and more complex themes, particularly the theme of judgment.

Judgment is always a determination of good and evil. This is not the end, but rather the way through. To determine good and evil is the consummation and fulfillment of existence—but not its end. Existence does not stop with judgment, but it truly begins. Something the same can be said for history. In one classical sense history begins and is composed of the choices (judgments) made, and is a record of those particular choices as opposed to a set of possible other choices. Each choice (judgment) made reverberates down through history, forever changing the options from that point on.

In the literature of existential interpretation which has proliferated since Bultmann's inaugural article on demythologization,[28] the theme of judgment has been laid bare inside and outside the Bible—all the way from Adam and Eve's choice in the Garden of Eden to the choice each person makes at the moment of death. But there is one final step to be taken to close the circle: to see in the final judgment the mirror and fulfillment begun so haltingly and inadequately in the judgment made by Adam and Eve. The Bible begins and ends with story—as indeed it only can. But the story of the beginning and the end treat of the same theme and arise in response to the same existential problem: who makes the final determination about good and evil? The choice Adam and Eve make in the beginning is taken up again in the end and re-solved. And the judgment made in the end reverberates not only down through future history, but also down through past. It brings history to a completion, to a fullness it never before possessed.

The real existential problem is not whether or not to do evil; it is rather how is it possible to determine what is good and what is evil. This is what history is all about, once we get past history as a simple record of choices made and deeds done. All existing histories are necessarily incomplete and provisional for this precise reason. The resolution (re-solving) of history, then, cannot come about in the simple, mechanical choice to "do good." History is not complete at that moment; salvation is not achieved thereby—when everyone chooses "Jesus as my savior" or any such similar slogan. History is fulfilled and creation consummated when the possibility exists to determine what is good and what is evil, once and for all. And to say that this is within the realm of human endeavor is to misunderstand the whole message and meaning of the Bible. Just as creation and existence spring initially from the word of God, so also fulfillment and consummation spring finally from the word of God.

It would be incomplete, then, to explore the recapitulative nature of apocalypse and limit ourselves to the explication of symbols—the serpent/snake, the river, the tree—or focus only on the final battle and victory of the Lamb over the beast. For we would thereby miss in the process the more profound resolution apocalypse offers: that we shall in the end have knowledge of good and evil. And in that knowledge we shall know history in its fullness for the first time. For we shall see what history and existence have been about all along. As the Bible begins with the problem of what is good and what is evil, and suggests that the resolution is beyond human ken, so it ends on that precise note, with God's judgment making it clear once and for all.

CHAPTER FOUR

THERE IS AN OBVIOUS DIFFERENCE between *what* is expected
in the future and *how* it is expected. This difference is critical to the
understanding of apocalyptic literature. The previous chapters have
by and large focused on *what*. It is time now to shift the focus in order
to examine more closely the *how*, for the precise manner in which the
future is expected bears on what the future means and how we live in
the present. In terms familiar to science fiction critics, the shift is
away from the extrapolated future toward the expected future. Thus
it is necessary to begin again at the beginning of the modern
phenomenon of science fiction.

From the beginning science fiction understood itself to be a
literature pointing to the future and preparing people for the
glorious vistas contained therein. Hugo Gernsback wrote this about
his first issue of *Amazing Stories*: "It is entirely new—entirely
different—something that has never been done before in this
country." He described the stories as "charming romance
intermingled with scientific fact and prophetic vision." They would
not only be "tremendously interesting," he wrote, but also "always
instructive." And he concluded, "Posterity will point to them as
having blazed a new trail not only in literature, but in progress as
well."[1]

The exuberance and enthusiasm which characterized this early
self-understanding has moderated somewhat in the intervening
years, but one need look neither long nor far to discover current
critical understandings of science fiction reflecting a similar
appreciation. The nuances may have changed, but the appreciation
of the social function of science fiction remains: science fiction is a
literature which helps people live in or into the future. J.C. Bailey
established the tone in the first sustained critical study of the genre:
Science fiction "has attempted seriously to foresee the new world
science is forcing us to face ... to suggest ways we may adjust our

thought, our lagging culture, and our statesmanship to face it with wisdom."[2]

This theme is reflected substantially in nearly all subsequent descriptions of the social function of science fiction. A representative collection of these is cited in W. McNelley's *Science Fiction: The Academic Awakening*:

Ray Bradbury: Science fiction is really sociological studies of the future, things that the writer believes are going to happen by putting two and two together.

Basil Wells: Science fiction, in its purest sense, should mean entertaining colorful fiction that either extrapolates what logically, or possibly, will take place in the future.

Diane Cleaver: More than prophetic fiction, science fiction is an extrapolative fiction. Future or past it basically constructs a parallel world, a world aligned in the mind with what we are now. Its concern is man and his reaction to any given environment.

Gregory Benford: Science fiction is a controlled way to think and dream about the future.

Vincent E. Gaddis: Science fiction expresses the dreams that, varied and modified, later become the visions and then the realities in scientific progress. Unlike fantasy, they present probabilities in their basic structure and create a reservoir of imaginative thought that sometimes can inspire more practical thinking.[3]

These random critical understandings of science fiction, particularly regarding its social function, are quite a bit more complex in their formulations than the grand exuberance of Hugo Gernsback. Although there is some overlap, there are basically two discernible trends which emerge: 1) future planning and 2) social criticism. John W. Campbell, Jr., a major influence in science fiction's first renaissance, provides one understanding of the function of science fiction as future planning:

If knowledge is power, then only by having more knowledge in the hands of the wise and understanding can we protect ourselves against the fanatic and thoughtless. Science fiction can provide for science-based culture—which ours is, willy-nilly, and must be, since science is inherently available by the nature of the universe—a means of practicing out in a no-practice area. We can safely practice anything in imagination—suicide, murder, anything whatever.[4]

Contrasted with this appreciation of science fiction as "future planning" in the manner of "think tanks" or thought experiments," is the appreciation of science fiction as social criticism, in the manner of "admonitory utopias." Oscar Schaftel sums up this position:

Probably the greatest service that science fiction can perform at this time [1953] is to continue to evade the official and unofficial censorship that has' fallen upon most media of communication ... that forbids satirizing bankers or free enterprise; blacklists and redlists are the techniques of inhibiting positive criticism of a degraded social system. In science fiction one can reflect our times in the mirror of the future or a far-off land, as More did in his *Utopia*.[5]

Thus, briefly, the claims made for the social function of science fiction: 1) that it helps people live in or into the future by enabling an imaginative practicing out in a no-practice area, or 2) that it serves as social criticism through the medium of the admonitory utopia.

From a literary-critical point of view, however, the problem arises: How do we verify these claims without resorting to sociological analysis and/or psychological testing. For only wholesale polling could determine whether in fact science fiction really functions socially as the above descriptions claim. There is little room in literary-critical circles for such kind of analysis. It may be, and perhaps likely is, valuable in the wider perspective of how science fiction does function in society; but it sheds no light whatsoever on the literary-critical study and ultimate determination of the literary worth of any science fiction work. Thus the preferable question asked by the literary critic concerns meaning itself. What do science fiction stories mean? And, how do they mean? These questions, moreover, are not asked in relation to outside studies, but only insofar as the work itself is its own referent, and the meaning contained therein is determined by the relationship of the parts to each other and to the whole. Sometimes, it is true, a method of determining meaning is advanced employing a distinction between the literary world and the real world. Kellog and Scholes, for example, write:

Meaning, in a work of narrative, is a function of the relationship between two worlds: the fictional world created by the author and the "real world," the comprehended universe.[6]

Without getting into a discussion of whether there is a "real" world apart from story, the presupposition in this methodology is that meaning arises from the correlation of 1) the story, and 2) what the story is really about. That is, to be meaningful, a story must needs point to something outside itself but within our recent experience. Since we are concerned here with the meaning of "future," we would have to say, paraphrasing Kellog and Scholes: "The meaning of the future, in the science fiction story, is the function of the relationship between the future created by the author and the "real" future, the comprehended totality of things to come." But this is impossible; for what characterizes the future is precisely that it cannot be comprehended. It is not "real" in the sense that this paper is real.

We are thus forced to consider the meaning of the future within story. The question becomes: How does story treat of its own past, present and future? More specifically: How does future mean in the science fiction story? The question is no longer simply what does the future mean. The specific object of inquiry is no longer genre criticism, sociological analysis or psychological profiling; rather, it is the temporal structure of narrative. The argument advanced in the following pages is that *how* the future means is more relevant as an object of inquiry than *what* the future means—particularly when the latter is reduced to social criticism and/or imaginative practicing out.

There have been a number of attempts made to delineate the temporal structure of narrative. With a view toward explicating how they fail to differentiate between what the future means and how it means, let me review some of these. Mark R. Hillegas, in a short essay on science fiction as a "cultural phenomenon," specifies it as a vehicle of social criticism. Such kind of analysis inevitably tends to blur (if not eliminate completely) the function of future in the science fiction story. This is borne out in his description of the three basic types which constitute science fiction as a vehicle of social criticism: 1) *dystopia*, which extrapolates existing tendencies in our world today, to warn us of what the future may be like; 2) *post-catastrophe story*, which treats of the collapse of civilization after a world disaster; and 3) *space fiction*, a story set on another world; the purest form of social criticism.[7] The fact that Hillegas completely eliminates the function of future in his final category casts doubt on his prior two categories, insofar as they would tell us anything about how the future means. If the third type, space fiction, does not in any way touch upon the question of how the future means, then what do the first two types have to say in answer to that question? Hillegas fails to say. One can only suppose the future to be for him a one-dimensional unfolding of events, necessary for the referent of the story to fall outside the story; that is, necessary for the story to give the needed distance. The distance in time, like the distance in space, is what makes it possible to refer the world of story to the real world. If this is true, however, why is space fiction any more pure a form of social criticism than dystopia or post-catastrophe story? And, finally, if it is our present society which stands in need of critical scrutiny, how can that be accomplished if a major question (namely, how the future means) is eliminated as an object of inquiry? We will return to these questions more than once.

David Ketterer's study of the "apocalyptic imagination" in science fiction presents us with another treatment of temporal structuring. Ketterer employs much the same vocabulary as does Hillegas, and ultimately also sees science fiction as a vehicle for social criticism. Nevertheless, in the longer study that Ketterer's is, he is more consciously aware of temporaral structuring. When treating of the plot in science fiction, Ketterer describes the progression through four stages: 1) dystopian fiction, leading to 2) the threatened or actual destruction of the world, 3) the post-catastrophe scene, and 4) eventually culminating in "the cosmic voyage and worlds beyond earth."[8]

Ketterer's description of this progression is set within the framework of apocalyptic imagination and literature, which is "concerned with the creation of other worlds which exist, on the literal level, in a credible relationship (whether on the basis of rational extrapolation and analogy or of religious belief with the 'real' world in the reader's head." Thus Ketterer proposes three categories of science fiction, depending on the type of extrapolation employed: 1) "A writer may extrapolate the future consequences of present circumstances," 2) "he may extrapolate the consequences following the modification of an existing condition," or 3) the writer, "extrapolating on what we know in the context of our vaster ignorance, comes up with a startling *donnee*, or rationale, that puts humanity in a radically new perspective."[9]

The correlation is easily made with the "plots" of the science fiction story, and with Hillegas' three types: dystopia, post-catastrophe and space fiction. Ketterer may indeed have raised the level of discussion and provided new tools for the investigation of his third category, but he, too, fails to inquire how future means in the temporal structuring of the science fiction story. Ketterer's tripartite division exhibits the same problem as Hillegas': the third category suddenly drops time and future as vital consideration. Whereas they figure prominently in the first two, the third, in a sense (and in Ketterer's own words) exist "out of time and out of space." The question which can be put to Ketterer is this—and indeed it is the main question of the present chapter: why cannot a new rationale of time and future be a startling *donnee* which puts humankind in a radically new perspective? Or, as indeed this present book has been arguing, why cannot apocalyptic be considered as the *donnee*? My purpose here is to explore whether or not there exists another way of talking about the future—other than seeing it as an extrapolation from present circumstances and/or their modification. To jump ahead briefly, I will argue below that *how* future means in the third type is radically different than how it means in the former two. The former two result from "conjunctive" temporal structuring (before/after, cause/effect); the third type results from "disjunctive" (now/nevertheless).

There is one final treatment of temporal structuring which merits our attention. Indeed, it sets the stage for a fuller discussion of the distinction between conjunctive and disjunctive temporal structuring. Robert Canary, in an essay on "Science Fiction as Fictive History," concludes by describing science fiction as a "distinct genre of speculative fiction—a fictive history laid outside what we accept as historical reality but operating by the same essential rules as that reality."[10] Here we encounter an attempt to treat explicitly of the structures ("rules") of the science fiction story, precisely insofar as these rules govern the unfolding of time and how time is structured according to the fictions we create to explain its meaning.

Canary isolates three distinct fictive histories: 1) linear extrapolative, 2) cyclical and 3) linear non-extrapolative. The first is the predominant mode of historical thinking: things happen, one after the other, by themselves or through human agency. The second, the cyclical, is used in science fiction to "permit the author to comment on current social conditions without the plausibilty problems of linear extrapolation." Things always happen in the same way. The third, linear non-extrapolative, is a questioning of the nature of historical reality, or at least of our "shared experience" of that reality. Things always happen, of course, but never in the same way twice, even to two people sharing the experience.[11]

The point to be made here, in line with our specific object of inquiry, is that the future never happens in the same way. We readily agree that the past differs according to interpretation; likewise the present. But the future, in the science fiction story, is all too often a "given," to be accepted as it is, and endowed with a facticity, a "whatness" denied to the past and to the present. The only way out of the impasse is to shift our line of inquiry away from *what* the future is, or will be, to *how* the future is or will be; away from what will happen in the future to how it will happen.

For this we need to explore now the modes of temporal structuring. In the science fiction story, temporal structuring falls basically into two modes, conjunctive and disjunctive. The conjunctive mode is exemplified in those stories modeled on the "before/after," "cause/effect," "once upon a time/happily ever after" structures of narrative causality. The disjunctive is modeled on the "now/nevertheless" structure. (I do not prefer, although others may, to refer these modes to the structures of historical causality.)

The former stories treat of the logical and chronological unfolding of events through the mediation of human agency and/or the similar unfolding of events as part of some inexorable plan or force of universal magnitude, knowable (in its effect, if not in its causes) through human intellectual endeavor and accepted either as fate or providence, depending on the particular point of view. The future holds no real surprises—for humankind is either able to creat the future or to predict it. The latter stories, on the other hand, treat of the unfolding of time disjunctively. The unknown, the alien, the unexpected, the sudden happens disjunctively; it breaks into the present and shatters present expectations. But it is not the future which holds the surprise in these stories, it is the present. For the future happens in the present—else it would not really be a future, but merely another present which has simply not yet happened.

I am reminded here of Robert Scholes' statement about the function of literature of (about) the future: "To live well in the present, to live decently and humanely, *we must see into the future*."[12] What he should have argued, I would maintain, is that to live well in the present, to live decently and humanely, we must see well into the present. To see well into the present is not only to see that the present possesses dimensions of past and future, it is also to see, if only dimly, how we ourselves imagine the future will happen.

Concomitantly, the test of any science fiction story is not whether the story helps us to see well into the future—or even into our present. The touchstone, keeping within the criteria of literary criticism, is whether or not in fact the story sees well into its own present, a present with dimensions of past and future. In order to test this hypothesis, I would like to engage in reading two current types of science fiction stories: the short range, near future, linear extrapolative story, and the post-holocaust, catastrophe story. The former would include *Dying Inside, Stochastic Man, The Sheep Look Up, The Listeners, The Moon is a Harsh Mistress*, and *Rollerball*. I have chosen Ben Bova's *Millennium*. The latter, the post-catastrophe story, would include *Earth Abides A Choice of Gods, Lucifer's Hammer* and *A Boy and His Dog*. I have chosen Piers Anthony's *Battle Circle*.

Ben Bova's *Millennium* shows an affinity to Robert Heinlein's *The Moon is a Harsh Mistress* both in its setting and in some features of its plotting. Both tell the story of a revolution for independence by the moon colony. But, whereas in Heinlein the revolution is undertaken to save the moonbase, in *Millennium* it is made in order to save mankind from itself. In 1999, the moonbase Selene exists as a quasi-military outpost for Americans and for Russians, each independently, of course. It also serves as a dumping ground for dissidents, a haven for research scientists, and a sanitarium for medical emergencies. Earth, in the meantime, has resumed its hostile, warring ways (after a brief respite which allowed for the cooperative establishment of Selene), and stands now on the brink of total nuclear war. In one swift series of actions, the lunar Russians and Americans seize Selene, declare their independence, take over the satellite missle networks of their respective nations (thereby preventing total nuclear war), and hand over to the United Nations the ability to control weather selectively (thereby giving to the UN the force necessary to maintain international peace).

The usual claim made on behalf of this kind of short range, near future, linear extrapolative story is expressed explicitly in the laudatory blurbs which introduce us to *Millennium*: "What happens in *Millennium* is not merely what is possible, it is to a large extent what is already on the drawing board." "Slick, snappy narrative, worthy convictions, all-too-plausible forecasts." ."Bova's novel hinges on the hope that somewhere, somehow, there will be enough people with enough vision to see beyond national boundaries and to act in the cause of humanity." The implicit claim is that *Millennium* will help people live into the future.

But the test I urge is whether *Millennium* helps us to see well into the present, by inquiring whether it sees well into its own present. *Millennium*'s present includes dimensions of past and future. Its past is our present: ". . . the eternal spirit of brotherhood and cooperation . . . poisoned in a world choked by too much population and too few resources."[13] But its future is also our present: "We have all wrung our hands about the United Nation's political impotence. But this [weather control] changes everything . . . . I'm not at all sure that we're ready for this. It's the use of force—a different kind of force perhaps—but still . . . ." Marrett, the weather control scientist from Selene, who is presenting this option to the Secretary General of the UN, replies: "Force is the only way to move an object." The Secretary General tellingly comments: "Newtonian physics . . . . You see? I am not entirely ignorant of science."[14]

The temporal narrative structure of *Millennium* is never able to shake off this, its own analysis of narrative causality. Newtonian physics is the model for politics as well as for science. And for all its passionate pleas for trust as the guiding force of a new world politics (Can Kinsman, the American lunar commander, trust Leoniv, his Russian counterpart? Can they together trust Frank Colt, the black, upwardly mobile air force major, sent to watch over Kinsman? Can the Secretary General trust Kinsman as the president of Selene?), Newtonian physics is the model for human interaction as well. Nothing happens in the story outside the framework of cause/effect, force/counterforce, attraction/repulsion.

This failure to see well into its own present (Newtonian physics, applied thus, results in a one-dimensional view of human interaction) issues in a future which continues without modification the present world of *Millennium*, except in some few accidental features. "Force is the only way to move an object." So much for trust!

The failure of *Millennium* in particular, and much short range, near future, linear extrapolative fiction in general, is that it takes present knowledge as determinative of the future—precisely because of the laws of extrapolation. This "closed" view of the future in turn determines the appreciation of the present, offering a "closed" view of it. While the ostensible message to the reader is that he should forsake the present in favor of a future based on trust, cooperation and international peace, the structure of the story, based as it is on the laws of Newtonian physics, prevents the future from being anything other than a "slick, snappy" copy of the present, based on power politics, military force and monetary might.

The post-catastrophe story, when submitted to an analysis of its temporal structuring, offers another view of the present and its dimensions of past and future. Here it is the past, rather than the future, which interests us. The ostensible message of the post-catastrophe story is that the reader should live without a past. For we are suddenly thrown into a new world without the means to comprehend the passage. Piers Anthony's *Battle Circle* will serve as the example.

Battle Circle is actually a trilogy, composed of *Sos the Rope*, *Var the Stick* and *Neq the Sword*. The story begins approximately one hundred years after the "blast," when the resulting society in North America has evolved into a three-sided social structure: 1) the Nomads, the warriors of the battle circle ethic, who are symbolic of present day consumers; 2) the Crazies, the curious mixture of academics and servicers, symbolic of the service sector of our economy; and 3) the Underground, the producers and manufacturers of food and weapons. It is the Underground, situated in Helicon, a man-made mountain, which assumes the controlling role in the new world. Bob, one of its members, explains: "What would happen to the status quo if the primitives really started organizing? Producing their own food and weapons, say? There'd be no control over them at all!"[15]

The stage is thus set for the chain of events which comprises the plot of *Battle Circle*. For the primitives do start organizing: tribes give way to empire, Helicon is assaulted, and the social structure disintegrates. Do we have here an argument for the necessary division of society into classes? The consumers, the servicers and the producers? That could be one reading. But a closer reading might lead to the conclusion that there is a fourth class which plays an important role in the narrative structure of *Battle Circle*: the Ancients, who are neither producers, servicers nor consumers. It is the Ancients, moreover, who exercise real control over the setting and the plot. Obviously over the setting, for the Ancients created the post-catastrophe world through the "blast." But also over the plot; for by remaining the Ancients, by remaining inaccessible to the comprehension of those who inhabit the post-catastrophe world, they are symbolic of the refusal to specify the passage from the world of the Ancients to the present world of the story. A (hi)story which leaves opaque the transition from one world to another is no (hi)story at all. Just as there is no way from there (the world of the Ancients) to here, so there is no way to get from here to any other world than one structured according to the three social classes of consumers, servicers, and producers. And in the end this is precisely what happens: Helicon is restored and the social order is re-established. The "advance" is that now there is a freely chosen, conscious mobility between the classes; whereas before the mobility was chosen by those in control, the Underground. Some advance!

The title of the book, *Battle Circle*, betrays the temporal structuring of narrative causality which informs it: The cycle. Without the dimension of a living past, and access to it through critical research and understanding, humankind in a post-catastrophe world is forced into the battle circle of history, doomed to repeat the tragedy of conquest, revenge and social engineering—all without an understanding of the forces which control those particular forms of behavior. Helicon re-established guarantees the system, the historical cycle; but one now more sophisticated in its technical aspects of control through surveillance. The dead past, finally, is to be used to guarantee the yet-to-be-born future. The omniscient narrator:

> The nomads were the real future of mankind. The crazies were only the caretakers, preserving what they could of the civilization the nomads would one day draw upon. Helicon was the supplier for the crazies. But Helicon and the crazies could not make civilization themselves, for that would be identical to the system of the past.
> The past that had made the Blast. The most colossal failure in man's history.
> Yet by the same token the nomads had to be prevented from assuming command of Helicon, either to destroy it or to absorb its technology directly. There must not be a forced choice between barbarism and the Blast. The caretaker order had to be maintained for centuries, perhaps millennia, until the nomads, in their own time, outgrew it. Then the new order would truly prevail, shed of the liabilities of the old.[16]

Just as the past belongs to someone else (the Ancients), so does the future (to the nomads). Such an understanding of past and future precludes an appropriation of either as living dimensions of the present. Just as the past is closed off, so the future also. Given the present by someone else, we can only give the present to someone else. With such an understanding it is no wonder what is passed on repeats almost to the letter that which was received. What does the reader do with such a view of history, which presents each existing world as the product of what has gone before, to be accepted simply as a given? Or, worse, accepted as an order to be cared for by the elite until the masses are ready to assume control and fashion their own destiny?

In both the short range, near future, linear extrapolative story (*Millennium*) and in the post-catastrophe story (*Battle Circle*) we are faced with a temporal structuring which is unable to verify the claim that science fiction helps people live in, or into, the future. To be sure, all kinds of social criticisms are advanced and warnings sounded; but *Millennium* leaves us with a closed view of the future, based as the story is on the laws of extrapolation, while *Battle Circle* leaves us with a closed view of the present, based as its story is on the laws of historical necessity. In neither story does there exist the possibility for the radically new, that which opens the present to other dimensions, that which allows the present to be seen from a radically new perspective. The possibility for this does not exist because in neither story is there any way for the radically new to happen. Ultimately, the future means not only the same *what* in each story (a simple continuation of the same "one damn thing after another"—to borrow Henry Ford's dictum of history—the politics of force or the politics of class); it also means in the same way (it must necessarily happen according to certain laws).

If, however, the radically new future is really a critique of the present, then by imaginatively viewing a future as described in *Millennium*, we would, in the present, work toward eliminating the politics of force instead of allowing science and technology to serve as the means through which force is employed now much more efficiently. Otherwise the force used only becomes greater and more difficult to control, rather than wiser and more humanely applied. And, after having viewed imaginatively a future as described in *Battle Circle*, the hope should encompass a future without the politics of class, whether based on birth or technological expertise. Instead, technology serves to reinforce class consciousness and role.

The one-dimensionality of *what* the future means betrays in the end the one-dimensionality of *how* the future means. In *Millennium* the future exists as that which humankind can create and over which it has control. In *Battle Circle* the future exists as that which humankind can understand and re-create, and over which it also has control. What the future means cannot be divorced from how it comes about. This is particularly true insofar as we see how it comes about in the story. It is called syntactical meaning, the meaning which depends on the relationship of the parts to each other and to the whole. Newtonian physics in *Millennium*, when applied to time as well as to space, gives meaning to the future as that which operates according to fixed laws. To know the laws (of force and counterforce) is to exercise control. The future in *Millennium* has a meaning within the book itself because it is extrapolated according to the same basic laws which govern the relationship between all physical objects. In *Battle Circle*, on the other hand, the future derives its meaning syntactically from the same set of relationships which govern the setting, characters and plot: the circle. The future will repeat again the struggle to create a perfectly balanced and symmetrical social arrangement, the symbol of which is the circle. The meaning of the future is enlightened repetition.

There are other meanings, however; and for these we have to go outside the story. But it matters at this point where we go to seek our relationships. Kellog and Scholes are correct in this that meaning is derived according to a relationship with the "real" world: or, rather, a meaning is derived: pragmatic. But the "real" world is the world of human experience. Meaning, pragmatically, ultimately depends on a relationship to human experience. Freedom, for example, means pragmatically because I humanly experience freedom. What the future means, therefore, also depends on *how* I experience the future, how it happens and how it comes about. It does not mean depending on *what* the future really is; for we cannot know what it really is. In *Millennium* the future does mean something, because we do have some experience of the future as that which we create and over which we have control. In *Battle Circle*, too, the future also has meaning because we do have some experience of history repeating itself—not in exact detail, but close enough for us to learn from the past and modify for the future.

Both of these "extrapolated" futures, and their many meanings, may indeed prepare us for the real future which rises out of the present. But there is another kind of future, hinted at in our discussion of the third category of both Hillegas and Ketterer—a future which is the purest form of social criticism and which is itself the startling new *donnee*. This is a future which breaks into the present and puts humankind in a radically new perspective. Rather than extrapolate a future which means according to control exercised over it (and which is limited by the very laws according to which it is extrapolated), this *donnee* presents a future which shatters the "laws" of linear and cyclic views of history.

It says, in effect, that there is meaning in the fact that we can hope for and expect a future over which we have no control in its coming to be or in its subsequent unfolding. There is an experience of future which is "out of our hands," so to speak. Most often this future is experienced only negatively: tragedy, misfortune, accident. Or it strikes us as being the work of fate, luck or chance: winning a lottery, finding a diamond, getting a scholarship to Oxford. Yet the fact is that we are, all of us, at various times in our lives, reminded in story and song and fable and sermon and testimony that the most ennobling and uplifting human act is to keep alive the hope in a future world free from war and poverty and disease and hatred and prejudice—even though (and perhaps precisely because) we do not know how to make it come about and have never had any direct personal experience of such a world.

Let us return to our prior discussion of the meaning of the future according to the paraphrase of Kellog and Scholes: "The meaning of the future, in the science fiction story, is a function of the relationship between the future created by the author and the real future, the comprehended totality of things to come." It is possible now, in light of the above analysis, to make one minor change in that paraphrase, and so summarize how and what the future means in the science fiction story. It is "a function of the relationship between the future created by the author and the expected future, the desired totality of things to come."

Thus, when the story's future accords with our knowledge of the future unfolding according to scientific extrapolation, then the future has meaning. When it accords with our knowledge of a future derived from past analogies, then it also has meaning. But, and here we must introduce a third possibility if we are to remain true to human experience, when the story's future accords with our expectation of the coming of the radically new—without precedent in personal or collective history—then the future also has meaning.

It is this third possibility which I have sought to isolate, for the very reason that it enables us to overcome the views of a closed future and a closed present—the pitfalls inherent in the first two. The third possibility, of course, has pitfalls of its own. The remainder of this chapter and the two chapters following will concern themselves above all with a discussion of the dangers inherent in a view of the future as the expectation of the radically new. The danger consists, basically, in adopting a passive attitude toward life, dropping out of responsible political activity, and waiting for someone (or something) else to save us. In classical biblical and theological categories this is covered in the debate between prophecy and apocalyptic. Prophecy is presented as the responsible stance taken by the believer toward this world and its politics, demanding concern for oppressive conditions and involvement in their eradication. Apocalyptic, on the other hand, is presented as the irresponsible option, chosen by the believer when faced with those same conditions. Prophecy, that is, is based on the first two expectations of the future, while apocalyptic is based on the third. In the following pages I will be offering an alternative reading of apocalyptic, based both on the analysis presented in the first three chapters of this work and on an ongoing dialectical comparison of prophecy with apocalyptic.

Anyone who has read in the fields of apocalyptic, outside the narrow confines of textual analysis, has run across Martin Buber's scheme summarizing the irreconcilable gulf between the prophecy and the apocalyptic world view.[17]

	Prophecy	*Apocalyptic*
Eschatology	Native, Monistic	Foreign, Dualistic
Object of Hope	Fulfillment of creation	Destruction of creation, coming of new
Judgment	Revocable, conditioned	Final, determined

The problem with this model and its complete rejection of apocalyptic (as with all value-loaded models) is that it leaves no means whereby to appropriate the apocalyptic world view, a world view which Ernest Kasemann, on the one hand, has called the "Mother of Christian theology,"[18] and Frank Kermode, on the other, has called the "radical instance" of our fictions about the world, and a "source of others," including much of Western literature.[19] At the same time, Buber's model inflates the meaning and importance of prophecy, placing on it a burden which no one world view should have to carry.

For these reasons I prefer as a starting point for our dialectical comparison the value-free model proposed by Paul D. Hanson.[20]

Prophetic Eschatology	Apocalyptic Eschatology
A prophetic announcement	A disclosure (usually esoteric)
to the nation	to the elect
of the divine plan	of a cosmic vision of
for Israel and the world	Yahweh's sovereignty
witnessed by the prophet	as he acts to deliver
unfolding in the	the faithful,
divine council	
and translated into terms of	no longer disclosed in terms of
plain history	plain history
real politics	real politics and
and human instrumentality.	human instrumentality
	because of a pessimistic view
	of reality
	due to post-exilic conditions.

Its simple advantage is not that it is correct but that it works. It does not necessitate a final confrontation, battle and banishment of either prophecy or apocalyptic (usually the latter) to the realms of the religiously fanatic, philosophically esoteric, politically naive and irresponsible, or literarily bizarre. Instead it allows for dialectic which can be engaged in on many levels: chosen people/faithful remnant, spoken word/written text, monarchy/theocracy, Day of the Lord/Day of Judgment, or using Buber's categories: monistic/dualistic, native/foreign, fulfillment/destruction, conditional/determined, and so forth. I will concern myself primarily in the pages following with the dialectic carried on between the political/a-political symbolization in contemporary prophetic and apocalyptic narrative models. Thus the analysis hinges on Hanson's "translated into" as contrasted with "no longer disclosed in terms of" plain history, real politics and human instrumentality. The question, in short, is this: when the nation moves from political crisis to political crisis in a crescendo of frenzied activity, how does imagination's leap to the final *denouement* draw the specifics of history's path? Not: Is there hope and/or reason for hope? Both prophecy and apocalyptic say yes to the question. But: What form does that hope give to present life (to plain history, real politics, and human instrumentality) in light of how it ends?

More specific still: Is history continuous, and human life symbolically structured as *breakthrough*, demanding in the end involvement in the public political arena and the necessity of hard, dirty work to bring it off? Or: Is history discontinuous, with *breakdown* as the formative symbol, suggesting in the end disengagement from the present political forms and patient waiting for the radically new? Thus I present a third schema, wherein the contrast between prophecy and apocalyptic is explored through the symbolic structure and the moral message of contemporary narrative models.

	Prophecy (Utopia)	Apocalyptic (End of the World)
Historical End	Continuous; ability to create, reach	Discontinuous; given, coming on its own
Story (Symbolic strucuture)	Breakthrough to new life as reward; activity	Breakdown. New life as gift; passivity
Personal Life (Virtues advocated)	Moral uprightness before the Law (God's or Nature's), needed to make society work	Obedience, long-suffering, patience, needed to endure the coming hard times
Public Life	Involvement; response to God's promises and/or humankind's desires	Disengagement; response to God's judgment and/or judgment of history

The narrative models used to explore the contrast are noted above: utopia, as secular child of prophecy, and "End of the world" story, as secular child of apocalyptic. As to the arguments making the case for the respective lineage of each, I refer the reader to a previously published work: *Apocalypse and Science Fiction: A Dialectic of Religious and Secular Soteriologies*.[21] The proposal here is that reading utopia as prophecy and "end of the world" story as apocalyptic, opens both prophecy and apocalyptic, as encountered in their biblical settings, to new possibilities of meaning. And, I must make my own particular interests clear, giving apocalyptic and its child, "End of the world" story, an equal platform allows apocalyptic to critique prophecy in its failure to take account of its own presuppositions. I should add, finally, that the third schematic presents ideal characteristics; there is no attempt to present either prophecy or apocalyptic as the one correct symbolic structure of history and the proper moral response, with the consequent rejection of the other. Nor is there any suggestion that either of the two types appears in reality in its pure form. Nonetheless, we do label stories as utopian and as "End of the world" stories (e.g., catastrophe, doomsday, Armageddon, etc.). We ought, therefore, to be able to list those characteristics which account for the differences between the two categories, and account for the category itself. The schematic attempts just that, always being mindful that each characteristic is actually on a continuum on which there is an infinite number of points.

The representative stories of utopia and "End of the world" I have chosen have been selected for their clear representation of the extremes in each of the characteristics comprising the schema. I realize that to force them into the model does an injustice; but any critical reading runs this risk. The final test remains whether, having made the dissection, a deeper appreciation and understanding results; whether, having narrowed the focus, entry is gained ultimately into a wider perspective.

Ecotopia by Ernest Callenbach, and *The Dispossed* by Ursula LeGuin are stories representing the utopian model, as descendant of prophecy. As such they present a model of (political) history which is continuous, symbolized by breakthrough, requiring a personal life-style of hard work and moral uprightness before the Law, and a public response of political involvement as response to humankind's desire to reach perfection. *Love in the Ruins* by Walker Percy and

The Four-Gated City by Doris Lessing are the "End of the world" stories, contemporary descendants of apocalyptic. Their representation of (political) history is discontinuous, symbolized by breakdown, demanding a personal lifestyle of patience and suffering needed to endure the coming hard times, and a public response of disengagement from the political arena which now lives under the judgment of history. A brief recounting of each story will set the framework for the subsequent dialectical comparison of the two models.

Ecotopia is the story of a utopian state comprised of Washington, Oregon and Northern California, which secedes from these United States in 1980, totally isolates itself for 19 years, and finally allows Will Weston, a reporter, to visit and describe for American readers what life is actually like inside this mysterious country. Weston discovers a country entirely run on ecological principles (renewable energy sources and recycling processes), personalistic, self-fulfillment psychologies, and cooperative economic and political practices and structures. Weston also discovers, as revealed in journal entries which alternate with the collected columns, that he is attacted to, agrees with, and eventually converts to the ecotopian life, choosing in the end to remain there rather than return "home."

The Dispossessed is the story of Annares, the utopian world built by the Edonians, the dispossessed exiles from the parent world of Urras. Anarchistic, it features less political structure than Ecotopia; but it, too, has isolated itself from other societies, for 200 years allowing only industrial trade with Urras and exchange of ideas on the level of pure theory—physics, in this case. Shevek, a physicist on Annares, disconcerted initially, and finally alienated by the creeping centralization of the Production Distribution Center of Annares and the pressures for conformity in the cultural and intellectual life, stows away on a rocket for Urras in order to breach the wall which separates Annares (the future, the hope) from Urras (the past, the roots). Each world needs the other; but both together also need insertion into a wider and far more comprehensive political and cultural history. Shevek's eventual breakthrough to a "unified temporal theory" and his gift of the knowledge to the total galactic civilization allows for the breaching of all walls—past, present and future—through the means of instantaneous communication.

Love in the Ruins is a story of these United States in the near future, when the president is an integrationist Mormon, married to a liberated Catholic, and the vice-president is a Southern Baptist knothead, married to a conservative Unitarian; when the Catholic church is split into the American and the Dutch Schismatic branches and the faithful Roman Catholic remnant; when the political parties are the Knotheads and the New Left; and when man himself/herself is split into angel and beast. Borrowing from W.B. Yeats' "The Second Coming," Dr. Thomas More, a genial alcoholic, brilliantly insane doctor, whose wife runs off with an Anglican guru, concludes: "The center did not hold." More's solution to the general collapse is to invent the "lapsometer," an electronic device which can diagnose the malady plaguing humankind and, with a little help from the "underworld" figures, heal the split. Needless to say, salvation does not come through the machinations of More; indeed, his efforts end in a debacle of comic-tragic proportions. In the end More marries his lusty Presbyterian nurse, withdraws to Honey Island swamp to raise a family, and treats rich women at his "fat" clinic. All the rest— politics, church, business, science and so forth—continues much as before.

The Four-Gated City is a story of Britain's near past and near future. Set in London, it chronicles the post WWII ennui and chaos in public and private life. More specifically, it is the final chapter in the "education" of Martha Quest, the central figure in the "Children of Violence" series. The story explores the world of bizarre sexual life styles, the communist witch hunts mirroring the McCarthyism in our own country, the rising fear and eventual disgust with the policy of nuclear deterrence, and the practice of typing, categorizing and drugging the "insane." It culminates in a general hopelessness which looks to deliverance from all of the above through an evolutionary leap to a new humankind possessed with para-normal powers. In an appendix to the story proper, the worst has indeed happened: the world 40 years hence is recovering from biological/nuclear ruin (which, and whether intentional, is never clarified). Martha Quest and her fellow travelers (the faithful remnant) live in scattered, inaccessible and isolated communities, communicating through telepathy, striving both to develop those powers further and to keep alive the "true history" of the end time.

Our dialectical comparison will focus on the four categories at work in the representative stories.

Historical End: The symbolization of the end in utopian and

"End of the world" stories is not primarily a message about the end as such, but a clue to understanding the inner dynamic of history. If the end is continuous (i.e., rises out of humankind's efforts to create it), then the whole of history is understood as being informed by that dynamic. If discontinuous, the history's form and movement is neither directed by nor does it result from human effort. In other words, utopia is a story about humankind as the subject of history: "End of the world" story is about humankind as object of history. Try as they might, neither Thomas More, in *Love in the Ruins* nor Martha Quest in *The Four-Gated City* can effectively alter the given course of events. On the other hand, Shevek, in *The Dispossessed*, and Will Weston, in *Ecotopia*, as biographer of Ecotopia's history, cannot do otherwise than become bearers of significant historical change. There are problems in utopia—neither Ecotopia nor Annares is the perfect place; but these difficulties can be worked out in principle in the course of time. And, in the "End of the world" story, there are solutions and answers and moments of triumph— nothing is all bad. But in the end no choice, insight, or heroic action can succeed against the disintegration of civilization as a whole.

Story (Symbolic Structure): The story's symbolic structure, its principle of action, is dictated by the presupposed dynamic of history. Utopia's narrative is informed by the symbol of breakthrough. Just as Annares (the utopian society in *The Dispossessed*) and Ecotopia are themselves breakthroughs to new forms of social, political and cultural arrangements, so the narrative action centers, respectively, on Shevek's progressive series of breakthroughs to new levels of social consciousness and new theoretical insights, and on Weston's slow but steady awakening to Ecotopia's promise and his own conversion to its philosophical basis. Shevek's moment is described thus:

He was there. He saw all that was to come in this first, seemingly casual glimpse of the method, given him by his understanding of a failure in the distant past. The wall was down. The vision was both clear and whole. What he saw was simple, simpler than anything else. It was simplicity; and contained in it all complexity, all promise. It was revelation. It was the way clear, the way home, the light.[22]

And Weston describes his own moment:

A new self has been coming to life within me here .... This new me is a stranger, an Ecotopian, and his advent fills me with terror, excitement, and strength .... thank you for sending me on this assignment, when neither you nor I knew where it might lead. It led me home.[23]

For Thomas More and Martha Quest, on the other hand, the principle of narrative action is breakdown, both societally and personally. More writes:

The reason the Tang is warm is that the refrigerator doesn't work. Nothing works .... Don't tell me the U.S.A. went down the drain because of Leftism, Knotheadism, apostasy, pornography, polarization, etcetera, etcetera. All these things may have happened, but what finally tore it was that things stopped working and nobody wanted to be a repairman.[24]

Francis, son of Martha's lover, Mark, comes to an almost identical conclusion in *The Four-Gated City*. In the appendix to the story proper he writes:

The very first symptom of the general collapse was an old one: *nothing worked* .... the most striking ingredient of the early seventies was that nothing worked, everything fell apart—that is, from the point of view of ordinary living, where one caught busses and trains and posted letters.[25]

But personally also the symbolic structure is breakdown, in a literal sense. Both More and Quest (loaded names for the characters they are) undergo mental and psychological collapse. More concludes very simply:

Why is it I feel better, see more clearly, can help more people when I am crazy? Not being crazy, being sane in an insane world, is the craziest business of all.[26]

Martha's analysis, however, is much more replete with societal implications:

When they stopped torturing and killing witches, they locked people with certain capacities into lunatic asylums and told them they were freaks and forced them into conformity .... By these means the members of the population with capacities above normal (those people now considered to be in the main line of evolution) were systematically destroyed, either by fear .... or by classing them with the congenitally defective.[27]

Personal Life: Given the dynamic of history (continuous or discontinuous) and the symbolic structure of narrative (breakthrough or breakdown), there emerge at the personal center and core of life appropriate virtues, patterns of behavior, and survival needs, which both flow from and reinforce that dynamic and that structure. They are required not only to make the story work, but also to make history work.

In utopia (i.e., *The Dispossessed* and *Ecotopia*) the virtues advocated and the personal life style required to make society work are moral uprightness before the Law (here: History's and/or Nature's Higher Law) and hard work. Barry Commoner is quoted on the dedicatory page of *Ecotopia*: "In nature, no organic substance is synthesized unless there is provision for its degradation; recycling is enforced." All Ecotopian life follows this "law." In *The Dispossessed* the laws of evolution (Nature's Law) is also the law of history, structurally and dynamically. To a citizen of Urras, who has just quoted the old saw that "The law of evolution is that the strongest survive," Shivek replies: "Yes, and the strongest, in the existence of any social species, are those who are most social. In human terms, most ethical."[28] This higher law, moreover, is why change and adaptation, revolution and resistance to political power are necessary. As Shevek explains:

We've been saying, more and more often, you must work with the others, you must accept the rule of the majority. But any rule is tyranny. The duty of the individual is to accept *no* rule, to be the initiator of his own acts, to be responsible. Only if he does so will society live, and change, and adapt, and survive.[29]

In the face of discontinuous breakdown, however, virtues and values and survival needs shift radically. What is needed in the face of historical and political collapse is patience, obedience, and long-suffering—in order to endure the coming hard times. In apocalyptic vocabulary, waiting and watching. Thomas More, looking back five years after his "end," says: "Strange: I am older, yet there seems to be more time, time for watching and waiting and thinking and working. All any man needs is time and desire and the sense of his own sovereignty."[30] And Martha Quest, her liberal and radical causes spent, her fighting against the social and political forces which sweep back and forth over the land ended, her efforts at socializing the children made—now Martha faces her own life again: "I don't know what it is I'm waiting for—something."[31] At that point she embarks upon the patient, long-suffering task of "waiting out" her own psychological collapse (and subsequent breakthrough, lest we think these categories are absolute).

Public Life: This, finally, is the "real world." This public, political life is the real world, the way things really are. It is here, I suspect, that we find the real referent of dualism and the Manichean heresy. This public, political life is the "creation" which is doomed, condemned, evil, and to be abandoned. It is the world of Cain's city, Babel, Babylon, Rome, Washington, D.C., and London—all the efforts of humankind to make a name for itself. Or, just as biblically accurate, this public, political life is the creation of the New Jerusalem, the restored kingdom, the temple rebuilt, the axis of the world.

Utopia demands involvement in "plain history and real politics," as response to God's promise and/or humankind's desire. Shevek the physicist, the scientist, rejects the notion that his role is the pursuit of pure, theoretical knowledge. Having made his decision to go to Urras in order to breach the wall and open up communication, he says: "I am going to fulfill my proper function in the social organism. I am going to unbuild walls." Shevek has realized that

though only the society could give security and stability, only the individual, the person, had the power of moral choice—the power of change, the essential function of life. The Odonian society was conceived as a permanent revolution, and revolution begins in the thinking mind.[32]

Ecotopian life, too, is predicated on active participation in all decision-making processes: in family life, schools, factories, neighborhoods, economics, all the way to national politics.

In the "End of the world" story, however, disengagement from "plain history and real politics" is the resounding note. Thomas More's passion is to save humankind, but not through political channels. Reading Stedmann's *History of WWI*, More finds in it the beginning of the end:

For weeks now I've been on the Battle of Verdun, which killed half a million men, lasted a year, and left battle lines unchanged. Here began the hemorrhage and death by suicide of the old Western world: white Christian Caucasian Europeans, sentimental music-loving Germans and rational clear-minded Frenchmen, slaughtering each other without passion.[33]

In the end, however, More finds salvation not in revolution, change or political involvement but in the quiet center of ordinary life:

> I stayed because it's home and I like its easygoing ways, its religious confusion, racial hodgepodge, misty green woods, and sleepy bayous. People still stop and help strangers lying in ditches having been set upon by thieves or just plain drunk. Good nature usually prevails, even between enemies. As the saying goes in Louisiana: You may be a son of a bitch but you're my son of a bitch.[34]

Martha Quest, too, having battled apartheid, joined the Communist party, and demonstrated against the Bomb, in the end leaves it all to seek deliverance not through political action, but through intense development of paranormal powers. At the conclusion of the novel proper, Martha attends a party signaling the changing of the guard; it is the effective end of Martha's and her friends' involvement in British politics, scattering now to pursue alternatives. At the party Martha observes a closely gathered group of dignitaries. The final judgment comes:

> There it was now on the wings, ready to come on, gentlemanly, backed by the landowning landlording Church (its face, however, would be chummy, slangy, modern, tolerant) and Royalty, solidly and narrowly traditional (its face easygoing, good fellow, amiable) and all taking orders from America— not of course directly, anything open and straight-forward being inimical to the spirit of these ancient partners, but indirectly, through groups of international bankers and vaguely named and constituted advisers.[35]

The disclosure of deliverance, in Hanson's terms, is no longer in terms of "plain history, real politics, and human instrumentality, because of a pessimistic view of reality," due in this case to post-war conditions. The judgment of history has come down on Western civilization.

I would like to end this at the beginning. Martin Buber's schema takes on a new meaning if it is read as a value-free model. There are, in the end, two options which present themselves: the reformist option and the radical option. The correctness of either cannot be determined *a priori*; such a value can only rise out of the circumstances, the concrete social and historical conditions.

Almost everyone is familiar with the favorable reading of Buber's model for prophecy, and the unfavorable reading of apocalyptic. I would like to conclude by reversing that reading, drawing now on Hanson's contrasting description, my own model, and the brief look at contemporary models analyzed above.

Eschatology: Apocalyptic's eschatology, far from being corrupted by the introduction of foreign, dualistic elements, is actually a reaching out to assimilate those elements which complement and critique a narrow, partisan world view. Even dualism suggests, in a favorable reading, that evil is a cosmic force which cannot be reduced to one, particular earthly enemy, one nation state, political theory, or economic system—or to one religion. Fascination with native, monistic eschatology can lead to isolationism, exaggerated self-importance, and the belief that "our vision is the only vision": God on our side. Preoccupation with native, monistic eschatology can hinder the cross-cultural movement which fertilizes thought. Indeed, that preoccupation denies prophecy's own roots in Abraham and Moses, neither of whom was "native." Shevek is the appropriate example here; no matter how prophetic Annares is, it needs Urras and more.

Object of Hope: I have already suggested that the referent of the Manichean heresy (this world as evil) is more likely the "real" world of politics and the nation state, than creation understood in terms of human flesh and corporeality. The "creation" then of any political order is necessarily provisional; while the glorification and/or canonization of any political creation and the longing for its fulfillment is a manifestation of idolatry to be rejected. That is, when creation's meaning is understood as the present political order, then apocalyptic's radical option is the necessary critique offered against the canonization of the status quo. The object of hope is not only more than the present political order; it is more than a simple prolongation of that order, even when reformed.

Judgment: God's judgment (or, in secular terms: the judgment of history) is consistent, both in itself and in relation to eschatology and the object of hope. There is no final "escape" offered for the nation state which isolates itself, closes off contact with other world views, denies its own interdependence, refuses to acknowledge its own provisional character, and glorifies its own political processes. God's judgment or the judgment of history upon such a nation state has always been consistent—and is necessary, determined and final.

CHAPTER FIVE

THE OUTRIGHT DISMISSAL of apocalyptic hinders the work of practical criticism, not only in science fiction but also in the larger enterprise of cultural analysis. That the dismissal of practical concerns is based on theoretical considerations (i.e., apocalyptic is a corruption of prophecy) means that the corrective is not simply to accept apocalyptic in practice, but also to critique the theory behind its dismissal. This, however, leads to the greater difficulty because of the nature of the relationship between theory and practice. It is this difficulty I would like to address in the present chapter.

Theory always has some kind of relationship to practice. One current critical understanding has it that theory is reflection upon practice. Much of this study has been based on that understanding. From the practice of apocalyptic, that is, from the fact that apocalyptic is a mode of thinking about the future and its relationship to the present, which has been practiced for literally thousands of years, appearing and re-appearing at various times, sometimes more vigorously than at others, one can upon reflection develop the theory which understands and explains how and why it develops and what it means for people to engage in this form of symbolizing the future. This, in turn, is always tested against the practice, both ancient and contemporary. In short, theory does not rise from the solitary thinker sitting down and deciding there must be a new way to understand and explain, and thus a new way to act. It arises from a thinker reflecting on his or her and other people's actions, their practice, and from that developing a new way of thinking about it. As the saying goes: philosophy rises when the sun sets.

At the same time, the former understanding is also true: the purpose of the theoretician is not only to understand and explain, but also to create an understanding which will lead to new action. As another old saying goes: Up to this time philosophers have been content to explain the world; now we must change it. The point here

110

is to grasp the nature of the dialectic between theory and practice, and so understand the role of the theoretician. A theoretician must be a guide and a help, or, to use a very old saying indeed, a midwife, in reflection upon practice. The work of the theoretician is to lead people back to practice, not away from it. Theory is understood when practice is understood; not the other way around.

It would be a simple matter to dismiss much of the current theory about apocalyptic based on the argument that it does not reflect on what is really being practiced. But I suspect this avoids the issue. For the deeper issue is whether or not such theories can in fact see and perceive what is really being practiced. My contention is that they cannot. And that is the real issue. Most theoretical understandings of apocalyptic lead the reader away from the practice of apocalyptic, from its very existence and so from its meaning. To accept much current theory about apocalyptic prevents the reader from seeing what is really going on; and any further reflection upon the practice of apocalyptic is consequently impossible. This kind of theory, then, becomes a dead end. It may stand by itself as a self-contained, theoretical model, but it cannot lead back to the world of practice. More than a dead end, it is a trap; for any further reflection can be based upon the theory itself, or another theory necessary for its maintenance.

A theory which does not lead back to practice nonetheless leads somewhere—to other theory, to more theory. And the whole process makes another revolution, confirming in the process the primacy of theory over practice. When difficulties arise, more theory is introduced to deal with the difficulties. It is never thought possible that perhaps a whole rethinking ought to be done.

In the following analysis of the cases against apocalyptic I want to test the theories by asking whether they do in fact lead back to the practice—not in the sense that they provide a basis for the practice, but in the sense that they help the reader see what is really going on. This, after all, is the only true test of theory. My overall point in the chapter is that an outright dismissal of apocalyptic, on the theoretical level, amounts to a dismissal of a whole dimension of human "being in the world," of practice, a legitimate way of symbolizing time, history, future, past, human decision and so forth. The whole study thus far has been based on the presupposition that apocalyptic is one way of engaging in this symbol-making process. I want to explore how and why some theory prevents us from appreciating this fact. Thus I will critique the critiques of apocalypse.

Martin Buber: I have already noted the tone of Buber's discussion of apocalyptic: 1) that it is dualistic, determined, and unconditional; and 2) that it betrays a lack of historical consciousness and a virtual denial of the possibility of change. Buber's disenchantment with apocalyptic becomes clearer the more he compares it with prophecy, which beforehand he has established as the one, true biblical model of "being in the world." His own words portray the gulf between the two:

Prophecy originates in the hour of the highest strength and fruitfulness of the Eastern spirit, the apocalyptic out of the decadence of its cultures and religions. But wherever a living historical dialogue of divine and human action breaks through, there persists, visible or invisible, a bond with the prophecy of Israel. And wherever man shudders before the menace of his own work and longs to flee from the radically demanding historical hour, there he finds himself near to the apocalyptic vision of a process that cannot be arrested.[1]

The identification of prophecy with hope and apocalyptic with despair is perhaps unfortunate. But it avails us nothing to argue with Buber on that level, except to yield to the temptation to affirm that indeed humankind can pull itself up by its own bootstraps. Buber, to be sure, does not argue that; he speaks of a "living historical dialogue of divine and human action." But the deuteronomic principle (good is rewarded and evil punished) has become increasingly secularized over the centuries, and often amounts to the most banal formulations (e.g., the power of positive thinking, ego-assertiveness training, and even the defense of capitalism and the free enterprise system). In the end it is read back into the history of human experience, with the result that the successes of humankind are characterized as prophetic, the failures as apocalyptic.

Buber's position leads ultimately to the inability of the interpreter to identify with the failures of humankind, with the losers, the marginals, the outcasts. Conversely, such a position tends to legitimate the efforts at control (psychological and technical) over the course of future events, by insisting that humankind was created to be the "center of surprise in creation." The surprises, moreover, are said to come through humankind's choices and decisions. Again, if they are good, they are prophetic; if bad, apocalyptic. This may indeed be an efficient means of assessing past action, but it tells us nothing of the future; and it offers no guidelines for mediating the present into the future. Indeed, it is tautological: prophecy is good because it is prophetic; apocalypse is bad because it is apocalyptic.

What we have argued for above in various places is a continuing dialectic between prophecy and apocalyptic; a dialectic which, in terms of this specific issue, allows for an openness to both successes and failures, to winners and to losers; which acknowledges that sometimes in some circumstances there is nothing left to do but "shudder before the menace of [our] own work," to flee before a process "that cannot be arrested." Apocalyptic is not so much a denial of history as it is a denial of the exaggerated claims made in the name of history—especially when that history is described as being solely constituted by free human actions, decisions and choices. Such history inevitably concludes by making exaggerated claims on its own behalf, precisely because it is a history written by the winners, those who have prevailed and who have the power to dominate and control. Apocalyptic provides a counter to this type of history, in that it is the (hi)story of the losers, those who have suffered, not so much at the hands of a "determined" future, but at the hands of a present determined by the winners. Finally, Buber's insistence that "prophecy originates in the hour of highest strength . . . apocalyptic out of decadence," leaves the Christian theologian nowhere to go with the cross, the central symbol of the Christian faith.

Nathan A. Scott, Jr.: The theological-scriptural position which traces the decline and fall of Old Testament prophecy and its resulting corruption into apocalyptic has its parallel in literary critical circles. Apocalyptic, in modern literature, is the irresponsible, narcissistic doom-saying, indulged in by some of the precocious and spoiled children of an age which has provided for all their spiritual and material needs. This contention is the literary critical equivalent to much of recent liberal theology's ongoing exegetical critique of apocalyptic as a corruption of prophecy. Prophecy, following Buber's analysis, is the liberal theologian's responsible stance toward the world, toward "plain history, real politics, and human instrumentality;" while apocalyptic is the ranting of rebels and revolutionaries who have given up on the system. In literary critical terms, the writers of today have too often betrayed their prophetic charge.

The foremost spokesperson for this position in the field of theology and literature is Nathan A. Scott, Jr. His recent article,

"New Heav'ns, New Earth,'—The Landscape of Contemporary Apocalypse," argues the point in his always lucid style. Apocalypse is rampant in modern literature: "secret hopes," "releases from the contingencies of life," "visions of the end," "dehumanization and alienation," "signs of the beast," "mythological apparatus"—"Now it is this mode of thought which has lately come to be the great hallmark of that whole insurgency ... named the 'counter culture'."[2]

When we seek to interpret this phenomenon, Scott argues, we are forced back to the Bible; for there, too, the expectation of the End was central. But in the Bible, two strands have to be isolated: the prophetic mind ("... inspired by so profound a sense of Yahweh's immanence in the present that the human future was in effect conceived to be already contained within the present"[3]) and the apocalyptic mind. Scott describes the apocalyptic mind according to the categories of Buber (dualistic, a-historical, and unconditional), citing the essay of Buber we have just put to the test. But Scott goes beyond Buber and other scripture scholars by trying to isolate what it is exactly that constitutes the apocalyptic mind. His conclusion is "Infinite Subjectivity." First he describes the present scene:

... it often seems in this late time that the only way of rescuing ourselves from the universal vapidity is to lay claim to that "sanctuary in the heart within" and there to find the locus of whatever truth may gladden and redeem our essential humanity.

This may indeed be an adequate description of what does characterize some modern literary endeavor. But Scott goes on to read it back into Jewish apocalyptic:

Surely it is the case that the apocalyptists encoded their thought in so elaborate a mythology (of beasts and angels and fallen stars) precisely because the empirical world having become intolerably threatening and absurd, it had to be radically dissolved; and since the *consummation* was expected to usher in a transhistorical world beyond all hazards and casualties of temporal existence, it seems natural that this mentality should have found its most characteristic expression in a kind of atemporal *gnosis* whereby the adept was delivered over to a visionary universe—of infinite subjectivity.[4]

Scott goes on to paint a detailed picture of this visionary universe of infinite subjectivity—as it is found in modern writers, literary and critical. In these writings, infinite subjectivity gives rise to: 1) a disengagement from history, 2) a mystique of inwardness, 3) anti-nominalism, 4) eschatological excitement, 5) the techniques of polarization, 6) a psychology of unobstructed need, and 7) the politics of ecstasy. The writers he cites do fit the categories well: Kesey, Mailer, Charles Reich, LeRoi Jones, McLuhan, R.D. Laing and Norman O. Brown.[5]

Now, what conclusions does Scott draw from this analysis? Looking at this contemporary landscape, what is to be our course of action? Where do we turn for reassuring words? Scott's answers are illustrative of the bind in which liberal, neo-orthodox, and privatized religion and theology finds itself. Scott argues that 1) the church's mission is to be "in part that of sustaining a sense of the dignity of our life in the historical order." This order he had earlier described as "the concrete actuality of the socio-political drama." The church, that is, is to help us avoid being ruled either by our fears or by our hopes. And 2) that we ought to be wary of learning anything from the present day "Tygers of wrath," from whom litle help comes in finding answers to the boundless energies of human desire. Instead, we should pay attention to the "horses of instruction": "My own guess," Scott writes, "is that in the field of the fundamental reconsideration of the human prospect to which theology is now called, it will find in the legacy of such men as Karl Barth and Reinhold Niebuhr and Paul Tillich and Rudolf Bultmann resources far richer .... "[6]

Scott's suggestions are illustrative of how theory often leads, not back to practice, but only deeper into the theoretical maze. Instead of trying to wrestle with the message and meaning of apocalyptic as it exists in contemporary literature, Scott seeks to fortify the theoretical base for prophecy. And just as prophecy in the Old Testament was dependent upon the existence of the monarchy (i.e., a legitimate socio-political order), so in our day the theoretical justification of the church, the university, and the theology of church and university, must be undertaken. The theory in which Scott engages is a program of legitimation, seeking in the face of testimony to the contrary, to provide a speculative base for how things ought to remain. The program of legitimation operates on three levels: 1) It legitimates the church as a supra-political institution, or at least extra-political; in that the church is to mediate the passage of humankind through the socio-political order, without itself participating in it. 2) It legitimates high culture; in that the only way to engage in criticism of culture is according to its creator-oriented aspect. All culture comes down from above; apocalyptic is an attempt to lead astray the masses. And 3) it legitimates neo-orthodox theology as the existential response made to the proclamation of faith; in that the proper response today is courage in the face of chaos.

This, in short, is a theory which legitimates the "winners," those who are in the positions of power, whose decisions do matter in the socio-political drama. For this, after all, is what history is all about—at least for the winners. This blinds us not only to the practice, but to the very existence of the losers, and to the literature which is theirs. This type of literature is often referred to as "user-oriented," to distinguish it from the creator-oriented literature of high culture. There is not a strict, one-to-one correspondence between the literature of losers, user-oriented literature, and popular literature; but there are enough connections to warrant a serious systematic study of this matter. Such a study is beyond the scope of this short work. For now I will only say that it is hard to imagine what such an outright dismissal of this type of literature means logically for our study of the Bible, which is a popular, user-oriented literature if it is anything! It could mean that even when faced with an appreciation of its message, the message is dismissed as irrelevant—because it does not fit preconceived theoretical judgments. Following is an example.

Walter Schmithals: Buber's treatment of apocalyptic has far reaching influence; we also find it at the heart of our next commentator on the matter. Schmithals says of apocalyptic that it is a "racial de-historicizing of the present." He expands:

In brief: if by historically we mean man's power ever to achieve, in the present, historical decisions in which he himself is at stake in the midst of history, then we cannot speak of a loss of history on the part of apocalyptic. To this extent, then, the fact that a pre-determined past and a decision-less future appear unhistorical does not argue for a non-historical consciousness on the part of the apocalypist, since he does not in fact live historically precisely in that he relates all history to his present lot and understands this, his present, in a unique way as the time of decision, that is, in an eminently historical sense.[7]

The presupposition is, of course, that history is constituted by human decision. From this presupposition the argument follows that apocalyptic is not non-historical, it is simply a-historical. Schmithals goes on to speak of the "powerlessness" of the apocalyptist, and the fact that he assumes "no responsibility for the fate of the world's course," but only for his own course. This is in contrast to the religion of the Old Testament (read: prophecy), which "as a whole tends toward the ultimate establishment of the kingly rule of God," the "perfecting of creation," and the anticipation of an "historical salvation."[8]

Much the same criticism of Schmithals' position can be made as was of Buber's: the reduction of history (or historicality) to human decision and action allows no critical role for the future as the radically new breaking into the present. It makes of waiting a simple barrier and obstacle, instead of the creative ground for the coming of the imminently expected. Finally, it tends to identify history with the history of the winners, with those whose decisions have led to victory.

Yet Schmithals' further observations do offer a slightly more sensitive appreciation of the meaning, origins and intent of apocalyptic. While acknowledging that we can have no hard knowledge of the social, political and economic conditions of Israel at the time of the writing of apocalyptic, the texts do show that as a whole the apocalyptic circles were composed of plain people who were "without political and economic influence," and that these people did not "participate in the party struggles and political disputes within Judaism ... and consequently found no protection and no justice with the ruling groups." All in all, apocalyptic was "essentially a piety of the poor."

> One could, then, think of apocalyptic as having arisen ... only in a stratum on a lower social level which does not deny lordship in general, but has the expectation that the evil earthly powers, which politically and socially oppress the nation of pious people, must yield to the good, peaceful, and helpful rule of God. In both cases, in this version, people were raised as "knowing ones" or "righteous ones" out of the levelling mass of "subjects" to the freedom of "persons."[9]

I have quoted at length from Schmithals, because it becomes obvious in his work that although he does present a rather sympathetic description of apocalyptic as the (hi)story of losers, he still does not allow this (hi)story to be in any way incorporated into the larger history of humankind. More specifically, if, as Schmithals argues, the story told by the people "on a lower social level" (this "piety of the poor") through hope in the "good, peaceful, and helpful rule of God," allowed for these very same people to perceive themselves as "persons," and not merely as "subjects" (He means, of

course, persons subject to another. We would say, perhaps, objects.),
then is this not a part of the history of humankind, and, indeed, at the
very center of that history? Does not this raising of people from out of
the levelling mass of subjects to the dignity of human persons imply
that the understanding of history and historicality as constituted
solely by human decision and action ought to be challenged at its
core? Finally, what could be more important theologically, socially
or politically than a story which enables this dignity of the human
person to survive and flourish? Not as that which is bestowed by
"earthly powers," but a dignity which rises from the people through
their hope.

Here is seen perhaps the best example of how theory blinds us to
practice. Schmithals provides one of the most insightful
understandings of the message and meaning of apocalyptic; yet,
because of the theoretical understanding he brings to the study of the
Bible, he cannot incorporate it. The theory cannot be put to the test;
because if found wanting, it will need to be revised. Specifically, his
theory of history and how history is made cannot be tested; for that
would mean that prophecy does not provide an adequate theoretical
base. Thus, he concludes, apocalyptic is a-historical. It has some
meaning but that meaning has little, if anything, to do with history.
Only prophecy provides us with the theoretical tools with which to
understand and interpret history. The question must be put to
Schmithals again: why is not the understanding of apocalyptic
(insofar as it truly raises "the righteous ones out of the leveling mass
of subjects to the freedom of persons") a political understanding,
constitutive of history on the same level—if not in fact a more
profound level—as that of prophecy? Why is this raising a-historical?

The following discussion of the essay by J. Norman King will
illustrate what happens when the understanding of history as
constituted by human decision and action is brought to a reading of
science fiction. Not only does an appreciation of the losers and
outsiders suffer, on the one extreme; on the other extreme it becomes
harder and harder to see where God fits into the picture. I will take up
this point in the following chapter in more detail, arguing that the
existence of a divine being necessitates the existence of another time
and another mode of future expectation. Here I want simply to
explore the logic of the dynamic of history: reduction of history to
human decision and action ultimately leaves no room for God. No
matter Buber's dictum that human action remain in "living

dialogue" with the divine.

J. Norman King: When we investigate the field of theology and literature, we are hard pressed to single out significant contributions to an analysis of apocalyptic thought insofar as it relates to science fiction. Nathan A. Scott, Jr. limited his discussion of apocalyptic to that manifested in elite culture. I am of the opinion that he not only misread apocalyptic thereby, but he also misread the contemporary landscape. But even though theological criticism of science fiction has not explored the related field of apocalyptic, there are beginning to appear some articles on the role of the future as portrayed in science fiction in its relation to the eschatological future. J. Norman King's article on "Theology, Science Fiction and Man's Future Orientation," unfortunately, may be typical of the work being done. It presents a counterview to the whole intent and purpose of the present study. For that reason it deserves attention.

King begins by noting the "future consciousness" of Western civilization, how it has shifted from concern about origins to concern about ends. Meaning and purpose are still the root concerns; but today the question most often asked is, What future will man create for himself and his world? The creation of the future is pre-eminently humankind's present enterprise. The "past-oriented" age, King argues, is "pre-scientific." Further, it is this "positive approach to man as creator of the future which lies behind all utopian-style literature of modern times."[10]

King continues his analysis by correlating this secular understanding with the biblical understanding. The Bible, unfortunately, comes out on the short end. For it locates the source of evil in the past—Adam's sin. Although it rejects a simple conception of a dualistic universe (one in which evil is a co-eternal principle with good), still the "flaw" of the past is read into the "future creations" of humankind and necessitates future action on the part of God to overcome it. The primal good is not simply to be restored, however; God's work is always something new—that is, "the fulfillment of human hopes is pictured as a divine intervention coming from outside the order of creation." It is in this sense that hope in God reflects a past-orientation. The point to be made, King writes, "is that where conditions seem unchanging and unchangeable by human hands, man's fulfillment tends to be portrayed either in terms of an intervention from without by a force greater than man or in terms of the removal of man from his earthly realm."[11]

Rather than search for the quite obvious parallels to this phenomenon (parallels which abound in science fiction), King buys into the secular understanding of time, change, development and history. Thus he writes:

When the situation is drastically altered by the advent of science and technology, however, the above conceptualization becomes implausible and unreal .... The notion of a pre-arranged future ... strikes a bizarre chord. The idea of an afterlife ... strikes modern technical man as highly improbable .... Within the new time-orientation, no future existence which lies, imaginatively speaking, spatially outside or temporally beyond the present earthly scene and its astronomic environment can speak to man's experience ....
    Man no longer asks whether God will rescue him from this vale of tears. It is rather a question of whether man's creative efforts, successful in part, yet marred by failures, will lead him to reach for a "power of the future," a God on the far side of man's transformation of history.[12]

So we are alone, after all! Humankind's horizon reaches only as far as it can create a future, or create a future God! For any figure, or any God, it would seem, "can only be located as emerging from and ahead of" the present earthly scene.

It is difficult to imagine that such a profound misreading of biblical data could be based on anything other than an equally profound misreading of the secular, scientific and technological experience. King might be forgiven had he merely solicited his understanding of science and technology from *Popular Mechanics* and the like (although even these require critical reading). But there is simply no excuse for a critic of science fiction to pass over one whole dimension of science fiction, one whole body of writing— being discussed these days under the rubric of "We are not alone!"

Sociologists from the beginning have pointed out the obvious significance of "extra-terrestrials." We cite, for one example, Walter Hirsch's early survey of science fiction, where, in the last time period sampled (1946-50), "intervention by 'aliens' " figured in 28% of the stories as the means for a solution to the described social problems. Technology and natural science figured in 26%; the remaining six categories listed came in at 5% or below.[13] Andrew Greeley's review of *Close Encounters of the Third Kind* is a more recent example. His argument is that while the church has down-played angels and miracles in the Bible, science fiction has capitalized on aliens and scientific marvels. His underlying argument is that science fiction is a genre which to a large extent is "implicitly religious," since it is explicitly concerned with the wonderful, the marvelous, the strange. He concludes: "You can demythologize Wonder out of your sacred books, but you can't demythologize the hunger for the wonderful out of the human personality."[14]

Much more significant, however, than the fact that King's reading of human experience is so completely given over to the glories of secularization and the liberation of humankind from the terrible burden of the past is the fact that we have here a concrete example of two problems which have plagued the debate between the religious and the secular: 1) The more one tends to emphasize humankind's responsibility for, control over, and creation of the future, the less possibility (and the less desirabililty) there is for the coming of the radically new. In fact, as is evidenced in King, there is an explicit denial of the possibility/desirability for the radically new. And 2) A demythologization of the present, such as King is convinced characterizes the modern age, only displaces the myth-making process. It now appears in the stories of the future, as King himself would probably acknowledge. But it goes even further; it leads inevitably to a re-mythologization of the past according to the myths which give meaning to and ground humankind's responsibility for, control over and creation of the future. In this regard King also pays scant attention to another corpus of science fiction stories which treat of extraterrestrials who have intervened to inaugurate the human enterprise. The ancient gods, the stories go, were really astronauts from other worlds.

What we have then in the study by King is an inadequate hermeneutic of human experience, which is based on an equally inadequate hermeneutic of the Christian faith. Together they fail to appropriate the past and the future as critical dimensions of the present. The past simply tells us where we have been, the future where we will be going. Despite the "failures" which are unfortunate but unavoidable, humankind's "successes" dictate that it must assume more responsibility for, seek greater control over, and try harder to create the future, and thus transform history. In this lies humankind's salvation.

The article ultimately betrays an uncritical base for theologizing about science fiction. Briefly put, the acceptance of "man's future orientation" as consisting simply of responsibility for, control over, and creation of the future misses the profound point that the expectation of a radically new future is incongruous with that orientation. Humankind cannot have it both ways. This fact is mirrored in the literature of science fiction. The "We are not alone!" model of the science fiction story is more than a simple variation of the preoccupation with future orientation in terms of "future history." It stands as a counter-opposite to, and a critique of, the "future history" stories which tell of humankind working out its destiny through its own efforts. In short, the imminent expectation of science fiction as secular apocalyptic offers a critique of the reading of all science fiction as simple, linear expectation.

I will conclude this chapter with a brief analysis of the modes of expectation, from simple to disjunctive or imminent. At this time I would like to take up a passage from King's article in which he consistently misreads the argument of yet another witness to the message and meaning of apocalyptic. I dare say King is in the larger company when he enlists Teilhard de Chardin to bolster his point of view; but perhaps just as we have been viewing apocalyptic from a wrong perspective, so also Chardin suffers from an elementary misreading.

Teilhard de Chardin: In an attempt to retain some ties with the Christian understanding, and to integrate the modern secular understanding of humankind's destiny into the Christian view of future salvation, King brings in the work of Teilhard de Chardin. Of Chardin he writes: "While retaining a Christian expectation of the second coming of Christ, he asserts that such a divine intervention to fulfill human longings will occur only when man, in whom the evolutionary impulse is now conscious and free, has carried out that process to a sufficiently high degree."[15]

The vision King ascribes to Chardin could be labeled, according to Metz's phrase, an "evolutionistically softened eschatology."[16] Evolution is certainly a central theme of the writings of Chardin. Further, even more a truism, evolution is the dominant process of symbolization by which contemporary humankind (at least in the West) appropriates the processes of time, change, development and history. Evolution is a conjunctive form of temporal structuring, dependent on the dynamics of cause/effect, before/after. If this particular understanding of evolution as conjunctive temporal structuring is indeed what underlies the thought of Chardin, then we do have a case of "evolutionistically softened eschatology." Or, at the very least, we have here a modern example of the ancient dichotomy between time and eternity, wherein there is only one linear path along which time proceeds to its end, at which point eternity begins and stretches on into eternity. The latter, indeed, is what King seems to ascribe to Chardin: the Second Coming will only happen after evolution has reached its climax.

But is this truly Chardin's understanding? Is this simplistic transposition of human life and Second Coming into evolution and Omega point all there is to the thought of Chardin? Further, does Chardin view evolution as a simple process of conjunctive temporal structuring? Does he subscribe to the notion of evolution as a process over which humankind now has complete control? To begin an answer to these questions, I would like to look briefly at one particular essay of Chardin, and suggest perhaps there is another way to read his work. Namely, that his message is apocalyptic, not evolutionary.

The essay, "A Great Event Foreshadowed: The Planetisation of Mankind," is contained in the collection of his essays called *The Future of Man*. Let me briefly establish its apocalytpc nature according to structure, form and content. The essay begins with a description of a world in crisis (the time-frame is 1939-45). It is a description of a present which is impermeable to the promise that humankind will be personalized as a whole. Into the chaos—comes a "revelation," a revelation, moreover, which consists of being transported to a higher realm: "I can see only one way to escape from this state of uncertainty . . . . We must rise above the storm, the chaos of surface detail."[17]

What is revealed is a "deterministic" structure to the future history of humankind: "An Irresistible Physical Process: The Collectivisation of Mankind." Even the evil of WWII cannot stop it; in fact, the more "we seek to thrust each other away, the more do we interpenetrate." Everything works unto the good, according to the overall plan. Universalism becomes the central concept of the new world: "Collective memory, common vision." All this coalesces in the "Spirit of Evolution," the guiding principle of development, needed for the completion of the human race.

But will it come? "Theory may predict its imminent appearance; but have we in fact specific reasons for believing that it will truly awaken at the expected moment in the hearts of our fellow-men?"[18] That is, are we justified living within the horizon of imminent expectations? Yes! If we pay attention to the signs of our times, we can perceive that we are indeed living in the end time. We see the appearance of "Homo progressivus," "the man to whom the terrestrial future matters more than the present. A new type of man indeed." (Can we call him the "Son of Man?") We see this man emerging everywhere, unable to be stopped, and attracted to other similar men across all natural and political boundaries. "It would seem, then, that the grand phenomenon which we are now witnessing represents a new and possibly final division of Mankind, based no longer on wealth but on belief in progress."[19]

Thus the essay. Now, Chardin can be criticized for all sorts of reasons (naive scientism, shallow theology, an inadequate theodicy, a wholesale distortion of empirical data, telling a story which can only be characterized as wishful thinking); but one ought at least be attentive to Chardin as an apocalyptist before engaging in that type of criticism. One ought at least grant that he does not appropriate a naive understanding of evolutionary progress, and tack onto that, in simplisitic terms, a Second Coming, an "Omega Point," a "Planetisation of Mankind." Chardin's evolutionary schema, to the contrary, seems to be more disjunctive than conjunctive. He speaks as much of "coming, awakening, foreshadowing, and appearing," as he does of control and determination. And even when he does speak of the latter, it is rarely in terms of humankind who determines, but rather humankind who is determined. Further, as a paleontologist, Chardin would be accustomed to thinking in terms of aeons of time, immense, almost endless stretches. It is difficult to imagine that he would succumb to the mentality which equates the consciousness of evolution with the power to control it. And it is even more difficult to imagine that he would subscribe to the reduction of imminent expectation to constant expectation, a reduction which seems irresistible when caught up in an evolutionistically softened eschatology. The point is that the "Planetisation of Mankind" does not function in the thought of Chardin as the logical, chronological outcome of the inevitable progress of evolution; nor does it function as part of that temporal structuring to which evolution gives rise; nor, finally, is it a structural principle for action, outlining definite steps to be taken to "hasten the end time." It functions, to the contrary, as the horizon of present human experience—and in this it can offer a critique of what is happening now.

We have come now full circle; God, through the Second Coming, is back in the picture. Or, to put it more accurately, God is back in the story. For a story about the radically new demands the existence of a character who is not under the control of the characters who await the radically new. Such a character traditionally has been God. Contrary to the charge that apocalyptic has been a corrupting influence, there is a real sense in which prophecy (stripped of its "living dialogue with the divine," and in which humankind becomes the doer and the cause of history) has been the corrupting influence. Not only has it slowly edged God out of the story, it has—perhaps more critical—eliminated the possibility and desirability for the radically new. To be sure, apocalyptic often succumbs to a similar dynamic. In the process of its secularization (definitively documented in the work of Norman Cohn), humankind assumes the responsibility for inaugurating the new age by destroying the old. That is another story, however. The question before us now is what to do with this character God? How does he fit into the story? Indeed, how does he fit into history—if history is, as the secularized prophetic branch says it is, the result of conscious decisions and actions of mankind? Is there a means by which to introduce God without resorting to apocalyptic? This leads us to our final critique of the case against apocalyptic. As found in the work of Langdon Gilkey.

Langdon Gilkey: In his study of the interpretation of history, *Reaping the Whirlwind*, Gilkey isolates the ontological structure of history as consisting of the polarity between destiny and freedom. This serves as a prolegomenon to a discussion of the horizon of history: the faith in a transcendent God who grounds and is the condition of possibility for the structure of history. A systematic discussion of the latter topic is the task of theology proper. It seeks not only to explicate the meaning of theological symbols for today, but also, through a reflective activity, to interpret the symbols in terms of modern ontological categories. Thus a prolegomenon is necessary, to provide the foundational ontology.

Gilkey's basic argument concerning theological method is that theology is a reflective activity, "an attempt to understand in reflective categories that which is lived in religious commitment." But, he argues, we live a committed life only through symbols. Now, "a symbol, religious or otherwise, means to us only if it thematizes, shapes, illumines and directs our own actual experienice, if it gives form to a definite region of our life world."[20] A prolegomenon to theology, then, will expose the meaning of religious symbols and the religious dimension. Theology, on reflection, will interpret the symbolic meaning in ontological categories.

Certainly we must express a debt to Gilkey for explicating so clearly the two steps in doing theology. But there are some problems, I would argue, in Gilkey's choice of religious and theological symbols employed to ground his theological reflection. Specifically, there is a problem with his reliance on providence, and his dismissal of eschatology, as that which is the condition of possibility for the structure (the actual doing and making) of history. A symbol must relate to present experience. This is the bottom line for choosing providence and rejecting eschatology, as the primary religious symbol, central to the Christian interpretation of history. Gilkey does attempt an integration of the two in the latter chapters of his study; but the weight of his interpretation of history is clearly borne by providence: "Providence is the sustaining and creating work of God within the ambiguities of historical life that leads to divine eschatological fulfillment as the latter's presupposition and ground."[21]

How does Gilkey arrive at this position? It is founded on the bottom line of his theological method: a symbol must relate to present experience, by way of thematizing, shaping and illuminating that experience. In constructing a prolegomenon, Gilkey builds on the analysis undertaken in his *Naming the Whirlwind*, wherein secular human experience was described as being characterized by contingency, relativity, transience, and autonomy. All of these raise the possibility of the Void, or Ultimacy, as that which grounds experience. When transposed now over into the framework of human "historical" experience, these same characteristics raise a similar critical question: Is it fate or is it providence which grounds human experience as ultimacy?

Gilkey, of course, opts for providence; and he explicates this symbolic language in terms of a modern ontology, process philosophy, in which he finds the ontological categories most appropriate for his arguments. Providence, Gilkey argues, is the religious symbol which best thematizes, shapes and illuminates our life, and thus directs it. For it speaks of God's presence in the world as one who guides and "causes" the good to come about, without taking away from humankind's freedom. In short, it grounds and is the condition of possibility for the ontological structure of history (the polarity of destiny and freedom) without denying, by-passing or short-circuiting that structure. Also, it allows for the integration of eschatological language and symbols, in that it "relates unrealized possibility, the 'new,' to achieved and achieving actuality."[22]

Gilkey's critique of the insufficiency of eschatological language and symbols in grounding an interpretation of history and historical life is based upon the following points: eschatological language, by denying the "presence" of God (its God is "not the god of the present") subverts the very condition of possibility for present meaningfulness. "To move God quite out of the present into the future . . . is to divest present experience of any relation at all to the divine."[23] Thus, Gilkey argues, eschatological language violates the primary rule: a symbol must relate to present experience. Eschatological language and symbol does not, because its God is only in the future. Therefore it is meaningless and useless for theological enterprise. Gilkey concludes:

Thus, if our present experience be void of any experience of ultimacy, which is for the Christian faith an experience of the presence of God in and to our being, then theological language (even eschatological language) has no experiential conponent to its meaning; there is no aspect of our experience which these symbols shape into creative form and thus these symbols are to us void of meaning.[24]

The temptation would be to take the easy way out, to deny that eschatological language is ever (or ever could be) read as moving God completely out of the present and completely into the future. But we have already seen one example of just that tendency: J. Norman King's treatment of "man's future orientation." Gilkey is not creating straw men or women; for what King does is move God completely out of the present and into the future, thereby denying, by-passing, and short-circuiting the structure of history by reducing it to the free exercise of freedom. That is, history has no shape; it is whatever humankind freely decides to do; it just is. King may be faulted for his theology; but he is unfortunately correct in his reading of much of science fiction. A large part of it reduces the attainment of humankind's destiny to the free exercise of freedom. Gilkey's critique stands, on that level.

But, leaving aside for the moment the question of whether or not eschatological language is to be read simply as moving God completely out of the present and into the future, we shall inquire whether it is possible to affirm unequivocally that eschatological language has "no experiential component to its meaning." Further, whether "there is no aspect of our experience which these symbols shape into creative form." And, finally, whether as a result "these symbols are to us void of meaning." To answer in the affirmative, it is necessary to grant Gilkey's presupposition that the experience of ultimacy comes only through a phenomenological analysis of the categories of contingency, relativity, transience, and autonomy. And further, that the experience of ultimacy is the experience of the presence of God.

To answer in the negative, it is necessary to introduce one more distinction: that between imminence and immanence. An immanent God is present; the very meaning of the word contains that understanding. The experience of a present God is the experience of his immanence. But the experience of an imminent God is not, on the other hand, the experience of his absence. It is the experience of his presence in yet another way. God can be present both in his immanence and in his imminence. To make the reduction of imminence to immanence, or at the very least to fail to distinguish between the two, is what leads to the dismissal of eschatological and apocalyptic language. To insist that the only presence of God is in his immanence does preclude necessarily the position which believes in a God who lives (also) in the future, leading us on. But the imminent presence of God does not preclude belief in a (future) God who is present to us—in the very human experience of expectation! Expectation is the manner in which we appropriate the experience of the presence of an imminent God.

Expectation, along with contingency, relativity, transience and autonomy, deserves to be the subject of phenomenological analysis, some of which we will attempt shortly in the section below. Expectation, perhaps more so than any of the other characteristics of human experience it seems, opens us to a consideration of the historical dimension of existence; for it opens to the very heart of ultimacy which grounds and is the condition of possibility of our historicality. It does so because it adds to the dimension of temporality as such to the other characteristics. Further, a consideration of expectation, alongside the others and at their root, has the advantage of grounding theological reflection radically in the praxis of the people. Contingency, relativity, transience, and autonomy are characteristics of human experience which speak of a Void, not only in the sense of ultimacy but also in the sense of a chasm existing between people. These characteristics are predominantly personal, individual, anguished responses; while expectation has its roots in a shared experience. "The most real thing about us," W.H. Auden has written, "is that we are all waiting."

The Modes of Expectation: If expectation is the manner in

which we experience the presence of an imminent God, then it is necessary finally to analyze the different modes of expectation. Thus the conclusion of our critique of the case against apocalyptic leads us back to a consideration of theory. But this time a theory which is reflection on the praxis (waiting and expectation) of the people, and which in turn seeks to transform that praxis, not merely understand it. I will use science fiction as the model; since I have argued throughout that science fiction provides us with a clear example of a literature of expectation.

From the very beginning science fiction has understood itself as the new literature destined to usher in the new age. James Gunn speaks of "visionaries dreaming a better way," and of the "missionary spirit" of science fiction, which demands "an opportunity to urge salvation, a change in ethics or morals or religion, a new way of thinking or a new way of life itself."[25] Science fiction, in short, will be the vehicle through which humankind will be delivered from all the evils of the present world. "Posterity," to cite again the words of Hugo Gernsback, "will point to it as having blazed a new trail, not only in literature and fiction, but in progress as well." This self-understanding, and not the usual glib listing of science fiction's preoccupation with doomsday, Armageddon, or catastrophe, is the basis for reading it as "secular" apocalyptic. There are many other parallel themes tying science fiction to apocalyptic: 1) roots in prophecy, 2) revelation of things to come, 3) secret knowledge, 4) myths of origins and ends, 5) future history, 6) openness to the paranormal, and 7) salvation from beyond. These have all been explored to some degree or other in the chapters above.[26]

Here it is necessary to analyze expectation itself, and in particular the one mode of expectation called "imminent" expectation. Imminent expectation, I will argue, is the proper mode of expectation found in apocalyptic. Although it is not the only mode found there, it is the one mode needed to understand the praxis of its readers.

Before describing the different modes of expectation, I must point out that in this analysis I take a stance opposed to much current critical work being done on science fiction. I am interested more in expectation than in extrapolation, more in readers' response than in writer's intention. In theological terms, I am interested more in faith than in revelation. Turning the whole matter around raises the question not only of what to expect (of which extrapolation treats

almost exclusively), but also of how to expect a more critical concern
to the theologian. An exposition of 'man's future orientation," such
as given to us by J. Norman King, fails to treat adequately of
expectation, and thus is caught inevitably in the limits of rational
extrapolation. From the present there is no way (no how to) to arrive
at the radically new. Yet the radically new has always been expected,
from the intertestamental apocalyptists to the present day science
fiction readers. Thus it becomes necessary to posit a mode of
expectation which is imminent (or, disjunctive), which does not
depend on conjunctive temporal structuring: before/after,
cause/effect, once upon a time/happily ever after. But let us first look
closely at conjunctive expectation, both simple and modified.

Simple Expectation: In the language of simple expectation the
future is expected as a linear continuation of the present. All that is
known of the future is that it will happen. That the future should
receive any special consideration is foreign to the thought of simple
expectation. The future is "the way things will be," just as the past is
"the way things were," and the present is "the way things are."
Change is a fact of reality, not a function of human consciousness
and/or interpretation. Change results in a future which may be
different from the present; but that future does not exercise any
critical function in relation to the present. For change is a medium
impermeable to human consciousness. The language of simple
expectation is the language of a people without a sense of history, a
people who have no awareness of any depth-dimension in their lives.

Any familiarity with science fiction, its readers, and most of its
critics, quickly dispels the notion that simple expectation alone
could describe and account for its enduring appeal. The intense
longing for the new age, just as in biblical apocalyptic, exercises a
critical function in relation to the present. There are, of course,
elements of it in both. The writers of science fiction are quite
competent in reading the trends of present times and extrapolating
from them to possible future worlds. And it should not surprise us
that apocalyptic writers, too, were able to read the "signs of the
times" and from them project the impending collapse of the social
order.

But what a reading of apocalyptic and science fiction as popular
literature has to offer is the introduction of an element which both
presents a control of meaning (through a conscious appropriation of
change) and generates the future as a depth-dimension of the present.

That element is "promise."

Modified Expectation: Modified expectation takes promise into account. For it is promise which opens a dimension in consciousness (we call it time) and creates dimensions in the present (we call them past and future) which are available to us through memory and hope. Promise allows us to penetrate the reality we call change, and to perceive continuity as other than material identity and sameness. Continuity (in terms of memory and hope) is a function of human consciousness and interpretation. The language of modified expectation (which has been modified through promise) is, therefore, the language of an historical people. Prophecy offers the most consistent example of this language. Through the articulation of the promise, Israel appropriated its own history (its process of change) and became an historicized people. The prophets, by mediating the past into the present (through the remembrance of God's acts), allowed for the mediation of the present into the future (through the articulation of God's promise).

In that both apocalyptic and science fiction are closely associated with prophecy, they exemplify the language of modified expectation. In particular, the promise of the new age becomes the norm according to which to offer a critique of the present age. Memory and hope become "subversive" of the present order of things.

Yet it is in this very moment, and movement, where we see the possibility for yet another mode of expectation. Modified expectation accounts quite well for continuity, tying things together in terms of before/after, if/then, cause/effect. But if memory and hope can be subversive of the present order of things, the present can also be subversive of memory and hope. Sometimes things do not reveal themselves as we remember, nor happen as we hope. The present, that is, is not always the present promised. Oftentimes it is less than we hope for; but sometimes it is more. It is the more in which I am interested. In particular, I am interested in the expectation which allows us to remain open to a present which is more than we hoped for, a present open to the radically new. This expectation I call imminent or disjunctive. It is aware not only of continuities, but also of discontinuities.

Imminent Expectation: To begin: In the logical and semantic structures of the language of imminent (disjunctive) expectation, the meaning is often carried by such words as: but, nevertheless, on the contrary, however. We are forced through these words to await something new, a reversal, a turning around, an opposing viewpoint. There occurs a break, an interpretation, a shattering of the expected end and meaning. But this break is also a transition, belonging neither to the meaning which has gone before, nor to the meaning which follows. It is an in-between state. So also with the temporal structuring of this mode of expectation. Imminent expectation signifies a breakdown in the usual configurations of time as conjunction. It disavows a simple before/after, cause/effect perception of time and duration. It throws together by radically disjoining.

This has implications for how we read apocalyptic. The usual reading of apocalyptic is done according to the simple or modified mode of expectation, with the result that, in the logical structuring, the dualism contained therein is taken to read as God *and* Satan, good *and* evil, life *and* death. In the temporal structuring of simple expectation it reads: after Satan, evil, and death have had their day, then God, good, and life will overcome. In modified expectation it reads: due to the inevitable superiority of God, good and life, through their efforts Satan, evil, and death will be overcome. Both temporal structurings are linear projections; they can be measured by discrete points on a continuum of time. It is possible to tell where we are historically.

Imminent expectation forsakes that model. There are still the elements: God/Satan, good/evil, life/death. But they are joined disjunctively; Satan, nevertheless God; evil, nevertheless good; death, nevertheless life. Or perhaps the opposite. Just as there is no logical process leading us to expect that one will follow, rise out of, break into, or transcend the other; so also the temporal structuring denies any simple conjunctive or causal reading. It is imminent expectation alone which throws the two elements together. It is as though by waiting for the sunrise, we "cause" it to happen. Everyone knows that waiting does not cause the sun to rise; neither is one surprised when it does. The meaning of the whole structured event comes through the very waiting; that is, through the imminent expectation which makes the waiting a meaningful act.

Imminent expectation, thus, is a relinquishing of control over the logical structure of events and a refusal to be bound by the pastness of history, by what is given as having happened on a continuum of "same" time. Further, imminent expectation is a refusal to be bound by the future of history, a relinquishing of control over the futureness of events. In this sense it is a "radical de-historicizing of the future," in that it refuses to control or manipulate that future through the imposition of a theoretical model. More to the point, it could be called a radical de-evolutionizing of history and the future; where evolution is the theoretical model which radically de-historicizes the present. For evolution is unable to interpret the present except in terms of before/after, cause/effect. In evolutionary theory everything can be accounted for in the present except the radically new—either as given or as expected.

Apocalyptic, far from telling the reader simply what to expect (soothsayers, diviners, astrologers and the like could do that just as well), tells the reader how to expect. It temporally restructures the world by introducing the mode of imminent expectation. For only imminent expectation allows the closed fabric of time to open for the radically new. And the time which is closed most securely, ironically, is the present; especially when the present is seen as the sum of all that has gone before and the ground of all that will follow. Imminent expectation, therefore, is a "radical historicizing" of the present, this in-between time. But in order to prevent this transition time from becoming merely another duration, apocalyptic continues by telling the end of the story, in the same literary forms as it told the beginning. It does not end with a "nevertheless." How to expect is never emptied completely of what to expect.

The narrative structure and literary devices of apocalyptic bear this out. All narrative time collapses onto the present; the present becomes, so to speak, the navel of the temporal world. No matter who tells the story (Moses, Baruch, Ezra, Daniel, John) it is told for the present generation. There is no other time. The literary devices of visions, dreams and ecstasies (the literary equivalents of science fiction's time travel and parallel worlds) likewise collapse onto the present. One can go anywhere (anywhen) from here, now. But the point is that one must begin in the present if the radically new is to be expected.

Determinism also, long another foil for the critics of apocalyptic, is the narrative assurance that imminent expectation is not to be entirely devoid of content, that how to expect is never emptied of what to expect. But in the narrative structure it is significant that the what to expect is never human in origin, in choice or in resolution—it develops always from the mighty works of God. What is determined therefore is never humankind's response; the present remains open to the radically new. And imminent expectation is the medium for the breaking in of the radically new.

Finally, the how to expect of imminent expectation exercises the more critical function, and actually in the long run pairs down the what to expect until it arrives at a point similar to that of critical theory: what we can expect is the negation of negation. Some commentators would label the content of this expectation as "transcendence of death."[27] But there exist in apocalyptic much more than concrete images. Some examples:[28]

There will be among them neither labour, nor sickness, nor humiliation, nor anxiety, nor need, nor violence, nor night, nor darkness, but great light. And they shall have a great indestructible wall, and a paradise bright and incorruptible, for all corruptible things shall pass away, and there will be eternal life. (Secrets of Enoch, 65:9-10.)

The present Age is not the End .... But the Day of Judgement shall be the end of this age and the beginning of the eternal age that is to come; wherein corruption is passed away, weakness is abolished, infidelity cut off, while righteousness is grown and faithfulness is sprung up. (4 Ezra, 7:112-114.

This is God's dwelling among men. He shall dwell with them and they shall be his people and he shall be their God who is always with them. He shall wipe every tear from their eyes, and there shall be no more death or mourning, crying out or pain, for the former world has passed away. (Rev. 21:3-4.

These images are to be taken "literally"; that is, they function critically in the narrative structure of apocalyptic literature to prevent the "content" of expectation from regressing into personal revenge, individual triumph, and self-seeking gratification—all of which charges have been made against apocalyptic and science fiction.

Briefly noted, these are some of the temporal narrative structures and devices which can be accounted for through an analysis of imminent (disjunctive) expectation: Time becomes focal and disjointed; history becomes a matter of relinquishing control; the present becomes an openness to the radically new; and the end becomes the negation of negation. Much of this was also treated above in our discussion of the stories of Walker Percy and Doris Lessing.

One can only speculate as to whether the original readers of apocalyptic were aware of the inner connection between how to read and how to expect. But science fiction readers, it seems, were always aware of that connection. Indeed, I would argue that the popularity of science fiction is due as much (if not more) to this mode of imminent expectation, as it is to the scientific ideas, theories, discoveries or gadgets. In this regard science fiction is as old as apocalyptic, and as new as the "new" always is. Science fiction from the beginning was always a literature of wonder. The titles of the pulps bear this out: "strange, marvelous, amazing, fantastic, and astounding" were words used in many titles. The stories were no longer read simply as romances (although structurally they were those); instead, they were seen as testimonies of people who had seen the future, who had seen tomorrow. Time was no longer perceived as past, present, future, stretching along a logical and chronological line, progressing according to fixed laws. Time consisted of today (this present time) and tomorrow. It was measured not in terms of ordinary events, but extraordinary ones. Each astounding event ushered in a totally new age. It was not continuity which characterized time, it was discontinuity. Tomorrow was a new age. All the political, economic, social, religious and cultural institutions would pass away when the new age came—although quite obviously not all in every story.

As with apocalyptic, moreover, the how to expect in science fiction exercises a critical function in relation to the what to expect. From the start science fiction never capitulated to the temptation of settling for one particular formulation of the new—the totally new was always desirable. Thus the new worlds of "Doc" Smith (galactic empires) became the old worlds of Isaac Asimov; just as the new worlds of Robert Heinlein (*Starship Troopers*) became the old worlds of Joe Haldeman (*The Forever War*). The political is at the mercy of the cosmological; and both, in turn, are at the mercy of the historical—that moment of choice, of decision, and,/more importantly, of expectation which swallow up all the small worlds we call home.

In the literary critical study of science fiction of recent, the focus has shifted away from the world of "tomorrow": which people expect, toward the "future" world which the writer extrapolates according to scientific and/or literary laws and structures. In theological terms, *adventum* has given way to *futurum*. The subsequent temptation to domesticate the radical nature of science fiction's imminent expectation became irresistible. Just as it was done in the early church by the privatizing and individualizing of eschatology, so it is done today by reducing science fiction to a "head trip," a sophisticated version of science fiction as escape literature. We have, to the contrary, argued that apocalyptic (and so science fiction by inclusion, since it is secular apocalyptic) is a political literature. As such it calls all structures, ideological as well as political, into question. To this point, a critical acceptance of the mode of imminent expectation calls for a revision of the one-dimensional hermeneutic of secular experience which views future orientation only in terms of humankind's responsibility for, creation of, and control over the future. For there is no easier way to suffer the loss of the future than to domesticate its critical function. And there is no easier way to domesticate the future's critical function than to view it as that over which humankind has complete control.

CHAPTER SIX

BUILDING THEORETICAL MODELS is always a dubious exercise. Error is not so much the hazard as is impracticality; the realization that in the end the model may serve no useful function, but only confuse and mislead others from further serious study. The danger, when it comes right down to it, is that the model might be taken for reality. But an opposite danger is present when one refuses to build a theoretical model: that reality remains so amorphous as to be impossible to be gotten hold of.

For these reasons, and others, I have put off offering any one grand theoretical model to incorporate what has been discussed throughout this study. Yet at the same time I have been drawn toward it for the very reason that it has been present all along, guiding and shaping everything discussed, often in a vague manner but there nonetheless. Sometimes it has broken through, most visibly in the ongoing comparison of prophetic and apocalyptic world views, their presuppositions and their consequent social, political and personal lifestyle ramifications. In this I have been guided by the models others have built, especially Martin Buber, Paul D. Hanson and David Ketterer. It was not exactly their models which influenced me so much, however, as their method. This prevented their models from being fashioned as rigid, airtight simulations of what was really going on in apocalyptic, prophecy and science fiction—although sometimes they are taken as doing just that. The prime example here is Martin Buber's model comparing prophetic and apocalyptic eschatology. In Chapter Four I offered Paul Hanson's comparison as a counter to Buber's. This kind of comparison is where the real world of critical study must continue, taking the models and testing them not only against reality but also against each other. For these models are also the reality which the critic must work with. None of us comes to reality without some kind of model of reality already at hand to guide us in our first contact and initial stages of study. It is incumbent upon us, however, as we progress in that study, to make clear what model it is we employ—and even to offer some kind of critique of it, pointing out its limitations and its weaknesses, while at the same time taking care not to deny its insights and strengths.

The real test of any model is whether or not in the end it reflects the full range of reality and all its ambiguities, whether or not it can be argued from both sides. Again, Buber's model is the prime example. Although most often employed as a tool to applaud prophetic eschatology and condemn apocalyptic, I have attempted above to argue it from the opposite point of view—as I think it can be argued. It can be used, that is, to defend the proposition that apocalyptic eschatology contains a needed corrective to prophetic eschatology, preventing the latter from reducing God's will to human decisions made in history.

The model presented in this chapter, then, is only that, a model. Yet it is to be taken seriously, as an attempt to present fully the wide range and ambiguities of all the above discussion of apocalyptic and science fiction: where it all starts, how people have talked about it, what its major themes are, what effect it has on the social and political sensibilities of people, how it arose in times past and continues to arise in times present, how it is reflected in philosophical, theological and literary categories, and who are its main adherents, devotees and practitioners. Just as throughout the study I have moved backward and forward across different and differing ages, so in the model also. Likewise moving from the religious to the secular; I have in the model as in the study refused to be bound by rigid categories. Above all, I have tried to keep in mind the other one major theme of the study—that of the role and function of apocalyptic, be it sacred or secular: People tell stories about the future because they cannot live without some kind of story that continues on through, past the present. But there are many ways in which the story can be told; that is what the model seeks to make clear, without judging which is the one, true way to tell the story. Needless to say, the model immediately demands some kind of interpretation. Thus notes will indicate corresponding appropriate commentary.

1) The model begins with a positive appreciation of the future— the future as promise. Promise is what creates a sense of history and allows consciousness to appropriate time and the passage of time as more than simple progression of events, happening because of fate, luck, chance or the unknown designs of the gods. The roots of this positive appreciation go all the way back to the Bible, particularly to

	(monarchic)		(racial)	(universalist)
Current Horizon	Sociological/political		Technocratic	Metaphysical/Philosophical
Current Issue addressed	Crisis of Will Future is object		Crisis of Belief Future depends on present action	Crisis of Vision Future is transcendent
Current Eschatology	Secular prophetic Emancipation		Religious prophetic Redemption as reward	Apocalyptic Redemption as gift
Type of Deliverer	Secular Messiah Politician		Religious Messiah Technocrat	Son of Man New Humankind
Form of Society Expected	Political utopia Good will Good ruler	Dystopia Bad will Bad ruler Bad science Bad technocrats	Scientific utopia Good science Good technocrats	Paradise/Heaven Beyond politics and science

FUTURE AS PROMISE

	Future rises out of the present	Future breaks into the present
Biblical and theological categories	**Days to come** **Day of the Lord** **this worldly** *futurum*	World to come Day of judgment other worldly *adventum*
	PROPHETIC Plain history Real politics Human instrumentality	*APOCALYPTIC* No longer disclosed in these terms because of pessimism due to post-exilic conditions
Reading of past history and projection into future	*CONJUNCTIVE*	*DISJUNCTIVE* *UNIVERSALIST*
	Monarchic *Racial* Maccabean tradition Rabbinic tradition	Wisdom/Gnostic/ Apocalyptic tradition
	Restoration Theocracy	New Age

	(political utopia)	(scientific utopia)	(paradise/heaven)
Dynamic of History and Salvation	Salvation *of* history Deliverance through will to power	Salvation *in/through* history Deliverance by science and technology from all earthly evil	Salvation *beyond* history Deliverance of the elect from beyond to the beyond
Personal life dynamic in relation to society	Tension between individual will and group will	Commitment to work for "salvation" of all humankind	Company of elected withdraw from the world
Death: End of Life— End of History	*Physical immortality* Personal No end (as goal) to history, only ends, cyclical	*Racial Immortality* Group, memory End is fulfillment of history	*Spiritual immortality* Mind, one "life" End is passage to New Age
Tension of Creation/Judgment	Creation continued No judgment	Creation fulfilled Judgment conditional	Creation transcended Judgment final and absolute

	(monarchic)		(racial)	(universalist)
Type of extrapolation science fiction criticism (Hillegas and Ketterer)	*Simple*: future rises from present circumstances		*Modified*: rises from modification of present circumstances	(*Disjunctive*) Startling new *donnee* puts humankind in new perspective
	Other worlds in time and space		Other worlds out of time and space	The present world in other terms
Literary Style/Genre	*Realism*	*Dystopia Satire*	*Romance/myth*	*Mythic surrealism/Fantasy*
Self-concept of writer	*Prognosticator* (Heinlein)		*Prophet* (Asimov)	*Seer* (Clarke)
Projection onto characters of stories	*Will*		*Reason* Intelligence	*Imagination* Intelligence
Relation of characters to mediation of future	Future is mediated by decisions made, no reasons		Future is mediated by decisions made grounded in a rational faith	Future is mediated by the "radically new," not made, but welcomed in hope.

the deuteronomic writer and to the prophets. Both insisted on remembering God's acts in history and seeing in them a pledge of further acts on behalf of the people, requiring on their part memory, hope, some kind of appropriate response in the social order. As in the past, so in the future. Any people who have a sense of history do so because of some kind of sense of the future as promise. Without a tie to the past, stretching into the future, (based on some promise made and still operative), there is no history—that is, there is no story people can tell to make sense of what is happening now. The first and most important point to make, therefore, is that the future as promise is demanded to make sense more of the present than of the future. Telling a story about the future is always a way of telling what is going on in the present.

But not every story is going to be the same kind of story. Nor do the stories differ merely because the future is an absolute mystery and people can only guess what is going to happen. The future as promise functions in different ways; that is, the future reveals different understandings about what is going on in the present, and what has been going on up to the present.

In order to begin somewhere, I have chosen a distinction, made years ago by H.H. Rowley, between the future rising out of the present and the future breaking into the present.[1] This seems to be the most basic distinction to make, and from it flow all subsequent distinctions. It implies an understanding of the present's relationship to the past and to the future. It views the flow of time and events either conjunctively or disjunctively. And it contains already a hint of the appropriate response demanded of the people—active participation in the making (doing) of history, or passive observers to its unfolding. It is either a story of what people do, or what is done to them. Finally, the distinction contains implicitly the current distinction between humankind as the subject of history and humankind as the object of history. That, however, is perhaps to see too much at this point.

The distinction is deeply rooted in an appreciation of what has been going on up to the present. It is not simply a statement about the future; it says much more of the past than it does the future. It is an understanding of how we come to be where we are. Paradoxically, the understanding that the future breaks into the present is an understanding which itself rises out of the present. Just as the opposite is also the case: the understanding that the future rises out of the present is an understanding which itself breaks into the present. The point is that neither one comes about in isolation from or independence of the other. Prophecy without apocalyptic cannot understand its own coming into being; nor can apocalyptic without prophecy understand its own foundations.

The distinction, therefore, is not a judgment as to the worth of one over the other; but it is some kind of judgment upon the effort to choose one over the other. There is simply no way to reduce stories about the future to one or other of the categories. Thus, in the Bible, we find references to both, distinguishing between Days to come/World to come, Day of the Lord/Day of Judgment, this worldly/other worldly, and so on and so forth. The Bible itself makes no final judgment as to the ascendency of one over the other. It preserves both—even in the New Testament—choosing at one time to emphasize the continuity of history, at another time, the discontinuity. But closer reflection would enable us to see that this is really the way things are—or at least the way we approach life as a whole. We make no absolute judgments about the nature of history and how it is made. We are unable to specify categorically that history unfolds continuously based upon the decisions made by each and every one of us, whose decisions create and fashion our own particular futures. This is an utter impossibility. We know that is not how life is—and we have all kinds of stories, individual and collective, which tell it like it is also: accidents, breakthroughs, turns of luck, insights, windfalls, and so forth.

Science fiction, finally, is split down the middle in the same way. To counter the stories of humankind's progress of raising itself by the studied, logical application of scientific method and reasoning, science fiction also tells stories of visits from outer space, invasions of extra-terrestrials, and of "close encounters." Against the "future history" motif, it holds the message that "we are not alone." *Star Wars* is immediately balanced by *Close Encounters*. Heinlein and Asimov are chided by Clarke. All these examples simply reflect that basic, fundamental distinction between the future rising out of the present and the future breaking into the present.

2) Our two basic categories, then, are prophecy and apocalyptic. Paul Hanson's comparative descriptions seem to me to best capture the tension between the two; but not just in terms of how each views the future. In fact, to continue with our claim that stories of the future reveal more about the present than the future, Hanson's descriptions

have less to do with the future than with the present, and a re-evaluation of where Israel as a people stands in the present. So many trials had befallen the people, so successively and with such severity, that the prophetic world view, in the mind of the apocalyptists, was no longer capable of interpreting the unfolding of present and future events. The experience of the past had been disjunctive—a complete and radical disruption of the continuity of the Israel kingdom, glorified to be sure in the sagas of David and Solomon, but nonetheless exhibiting some kind of stability and continuity—and this experience of disjunction became the dominant form of future expectation. It became how the people expected the future.

Apocalyptic, the point must be made, is a new form of historical consciousness; not simply new content dumped into old forms. In fact, apocalyptic suffers most often from the attempt to retain the old content within its new forms. One example of this is the expectation of an earthly kingdom, shared with prophecy, but now occupying a time in between time, the end of this world and the beginning of the new. Confusion reigns on this point throughout apocalyptic literature, and accounts for the split between the millennialists and the pre-millennialists—even to our day.[2]

The focal point of this present study has been secular apocalyptic in our own time, particularly as it comes to us in science fiction. There is, in apocalyptic science fiction (generally falling under the rubric of post-catastrophe and/or "we are not alone" stories) a tendency to leave behind what Hanson has called "plain history, real politics, and human instrumentality." The latter, of course, only insofar as it operates within the field of real politics. This will be seen more clearly in the comments immediately following these, when we take up the topic of universalism. The point here is that this tendency is not so much indicative of future expectation (indeed may not be so at all), as it is of reflection on experience. Our time is no different than any other as far as undergoing rapid and radical social, political, economic, religious and cultural change. That is not the argument here. The argument is that apocalyptic is the response to reflection upon this reality of rapid change. It has been the response in every age—not so much as regards content (although the content has endured remarkably down through the ages)—but more so as regards the form which historical consciousness takes.

There is a message clearly given in the science fiction stories telling about extra-terrestrial intelligences and post-catastrophe worlds. And the message is this: Present understanding of plain history, real politics, and human instrumentality are clearly not so satisfactory when it comes to giving meaning to the present and to the future as it is hoped for in the present. The stories do not offer a clear alternative on the same level to the political forms now functioning; such is not their aim. They merely state that the present forms are not enough.

3) The categories at this point, and particularly the introduction of a division in the prophetic world view, are of critical importance. Let us begin with the division of prophecy and then move on to the theme of universalism, for one follows upon the other.

Prophecy, it becomes more and more clear, is in dire straights following the captivity, exile and resettlement. For it is left without the "real politics" essential for its functioning in "plain history," through "human instrumentality." It is left, that is, without the king. Following upon the great disruption, and after a certain amount of time for re-adjustment, it is expedient to pick up the pieces and continue on with history and the promises of God. But where to begin? How to re-establish the continuity? This is where and how the major split occurs, between those who would base continuity upon the monarchy and those who would base continuity upon the race. There are good arguments for both; and both positions are firmly grounded in an appreciation of the necessity for continuity. It is not a blind trust for them, however; it is rooted firmly in the promises made by God in the past. Thus in the writings in the Old Testament, most of which were done in this period of Israel's history, there appear different schools of thought—the priestly and the deuteronomic (later to give birth to the prophets), and also varied and scattered remnants of a royal messianism, particularly in the Psalms. Each school continually goes over the earlier ground in Israel's history, writing and re-writing and editing the stories which recall God's promises, especially as they bear on the continuity they are attempting to salvage.

The two main schools which finally emerge are the monarchic and the racial. The former collects and retells the stories of Israel leading up to the establishment of the kingdom, and argue for continuity based on the re-establishment of the kingdom. A complete and full restoration of the Davidic line is called for. The stories of the latter, the racial, treat mainly of the chosen people who, for a time, like other nations had a king, but whose real king was and always will be Yahweh God. A theocracy is the renewed form that re-emerges here; but the emphasis is on continuity, both in the spiritual base and in the physical manifestations of that spiritual base: that is, a real, physical, earthly kingdom will be established when Yahweh God comes to rule.

At this point the radically new appears—both as the content of the hope and as its form. There is always a certain amount of continuity, even in the most seemingly discontinuous of movements. It is no less the case with the rise of apocalyptic. Subsequent critical study, unfortunately, has focused on content, to the neglect of form. The content, to be sure, is dualism; and dualism has been the bane of all scriptural scholars and theologians, from the beginning down to the revisionist theologians of our times. If critical reflection and study remains focused on the content of apocalyptic, particularly on its thematic use of a dualistic world view and time frame, then there is not much hope that apocalyptic will ever be seen other than as a corruption of all that is noble and inspiring in prophecy and its world view—namely, that God acts in human history through the concrete decisions and actions of believing and loving and merciful people. That is, God acts in human history; but humankind is not simply a pawn in the games of the gods.

But the radically new (dualism) is also the form of hope, and not simply its content. The totally new world and the totally new age are not simply the objects of apocalyptic hope; they are the way in which apocalyptic hopes about this present world. Perhaps this is seen most clearly in the distinction made among monarchic, racial and universalist forms of hope. (Universalism refers to the hope of salvation being extended to all peoples, not only the Jewish race and not only through the establishment of the Jewish monarchy.) When reflected upon as an object of hope, universalism, as distinguished from either monarchic or racial hopes, appears rightly and inevitably as an almost totally fantastic, unattainable, illusory hope, which frustrates present political endeavors necessary to the task of clarifying contemporary issues and their practical resolution. Universalism as content is a red herring at best, an escape and cop-out at worst. It drains off from human activity the humane concern and the involvement needed to counter the forces of greed, chaos and individual self-gratification threatening always to destroy society. If universalism were only this, something to be hoped for, without a clue as to how it is to come about, then it rightly is to be scorned by those who read the Bible and see in it insights which to this day are as refreshing and as needed as always.

Universalism, however, is more than content; it is also the form of hope. And as form alone it is able to be of use today as a critical category (not simply an uncritical, positive object of hope). Universalism, when appreciated as form, says that it will not do to hope for the new in the same way in which we have always hoped. Universalism says not only that there must be a new object of hope, but also, and more radically, that there must be a new way of hoping. The old way of hoping simply will no longer be adequate. It is here particularly where the necessary adjunct to come, that is, memory, comes into play. Stories about the future, we have argued, are always stories about the present, what is happening in the present and what has been happening up to the present. Memory, then, is necessarily also a critical part of hope. A new form of hope will create also a new form of memory. Apocalyptic not only does not remember the same things as monarchic and racial hope; it does not remember the past in the same way.

But what is this new form of hope? Universalism, as one formative element of apocalyptic hope, says that just as it is ultimately self-defeating to remember in isolation, so also is it to hope in isolation. Universalism does not hope *for* so much as it hopes *with*. Apocalyptic, as one commentator has pointed out, is a "radical de-historicizing of the future." He intended this as a negative judgment; but there is something to be said for it positively. Apocalyptic, in its universalist motif, says that historicizing the future has too often meant one, isolated, "chosen" people taking responsibility for the future, and leaving all others behind. Universalism does not hope for a joining with others in a glorious future which we have made, and in which others will be saved whether they like it or not—or, as is more likely, damned whether they like it or not. Universalism hopes by joining with others now in a critical present which demands radically new responses to the old memories of the past and new hopes for the future. This is the new form of hope that the universalist motif introduces. Universalism in apocalyptic is not caused by the introduction of "foreign elements," such as dualism, gnosticism, and so forth. Rather, because apocalyptic is universalist it is open to these elements. It employs them because, along with others, it sees there is more to what is going on in the present and in what has been going on up to the present than the ordinary and accepted stories would (or could) pay heed to. As a result of this, quite naturally, the future also holds out a radically new form and a radically new content.

Apocalyptic, finally, is a way of hoping that keeps the motif of universalism alive in the Bible. Universalism is not new with apocalyptic. It had been present all along in many different stories and historical accounts. But apocalyptic is a way of remembering the theme of universal salvation. Thus the testimony of all the ancients (Moses, Abraham, Joshua, etc.) points to the presence of this promise from the very beginning. Prophecy, with its ties to "plain history, real politics, and human instrumentality," is always in danger of forgetting the promise of universal salvation, or else reducing it to the result of human decision/or engineering. The latter, of course, is the peculiar temptation of the science fiction utopia, as we will see shortly.

4) From here on it becomes even more complicated. It is only by succumbing further to grand generalizations and over-simplifications that the following categories can be developed. Still, it may be of some value to pursue the basic distinction between, first of all, the future rising out of the present (prophetic eschatology) and the future breaking into the present (apocalyptic eschatology); and, second, the monarchic, racial, and universalist categories—insofar as they can shed some light on contemporary understandings of what has led up to the present and what is expected to happen in the future. That is, our discussion will focus on the referents and horizons of current eschatological talk, what type of deliverer and/or deliverance is expected, and what type of society is desired to emerge in fulfillment of those expectations. All these will be explored insofar as they are manifested in science fiction, the contemporary prophetic and apocalyptic literature.

The horizon of science fiction can be spoken of as either political, technological, or philosophic. I have indicated in the chart that these correspond, more or less, to the monarchic, racial and universalist horizons of the biblical categories. It is not too difficult to trace influences down through the monarchic to the political horizon of much contemporary science fiction. This is most obvious in the science fiction utopias which are only incidentally derivative of some scientific or technological breakthrough, but focus most forcefully on the political structures necessary to bring about the glorious future. Much of H.G. Wells in the early days of science fiction, B.F. Skinner and Robert Heinlein along the way, and *Ecotopia* most recently have as their central theme the politics of the future. That their politics can be read as reflecting the age-old, perennial desire for a community of brotherhood and sharing of property is only another indication that the function of such literature is much the same function of monarchic literature in the Bible: the restoration of the kingdom. That is, its function is to keep alive a certain specific understanding of an idealized past, wherein deliverance is appreciated in political terms. Emancipation becomes the watchword; and political re-organization along the line of centuries-old longings becomes the means to that end. The goal is patently clear; all that is lacking is the will, the determination to get on with it. Political utopia is the creature of "will." The future needs only to be done—all the thinking about it has already been accomplished.

The corrective to this kind of thinking, however, exists as the reflected opposite of this genre: dystopia. *1984* and *Brave New World* are but two of the better known examples. The question which all political dystopias raise is this: "Yes! But whose will be done?" All dystopian literature tells us that the *crisis* of will (certainly a real crisis, and one which needs to be addressed in social and political categories) cannot be resolved by an *act* of will. To do so is only to compound and prolong the crisis. In the end it does not affect deliverance, but only confirms the problem, and necessitates another turn of the political axis: revolution. Real change, which revolution rarely is, is postponed until the conditions again present themselves for a radical breakthrough.

At the other end of the spectrum, it is not too difficult to trace the movement down through the universalist horizon, with its roots in foreign cosmologies and wisdom literature, to the philosophical and metaphysical speculations of another segment of science fiction. Here Olaf Stapledon and Arthur C. Clarke stand out as primary examples. Stapledon's *Last and First Men* scarcely differs in content or in form from the sweeping cosmologies of intertestamental apocalyptic. And Clarke's continued use of the alien intelligence, from *Childhood's End*, through *Rendezvous with Rama* and *Imperial Earth* to *The Fountains of Paradise*, gives him, like apocalyptic, the means to speculate on the meaning of human life and destiny. In both Stapledon and Clarke the theme is redemption rather than emancipation, the role of humankind being passive rather than active. There is no attempt (indeed, the message seems to be that it cannot be done) to understand humankind's meaning and deliverance outside a much wider and more widely understood and populated universe than the one under scrutiny by the hard, physical sciences, the practical politicians, and the highly organized technocrats. There is always more. Theirs is an attempt, it must be also emphasized, transcending the common everyday hope for deliverance from personal tribulations of poverty, sickness and the like, or the wider but still limited crises of city management or energy production by means of some marvelous new technological breakthrough which makes available unlimited, cheap energy. These are only occasions for escape from the rigors of philosophical reflection on the larger issues. Stapledon's and Clarke's work (especially Clarke's *Childhood's End*) radically questions the whole process of science and technology, forcing the reader to expand rather than narrow the categories with which to think about life, world, science, politics, future and deliverance. Especially of note is the radical questioning of politics that this branch of science fiction pursues. And in this, perhaps, the lines to intertestamental apocalyptic are most clearly drawn. If Hanson's phrase, "plain history, real politics, and human instrumentality," the rejection of which characterizes apocalyptic, applies anywhere in contemporary literature, it applies to this branch of science fiction. In this also it is a re-reading of the past, of what has been going on up the present, and is a judgment upon it.

The crisis, this body of literature says, is not political; nor has it ever been political—in the narrow sense of partisan politics. The crisis was, is now, and always will be a crisis of vision, of hope in a radically new future which will transcend any possibility now entertained by the individual or collective will. It seeks to preserve the ago-old wisdom (the "forgotten truth," to cite Huston Smith's timely study) that "we are not alone."[3] This is the 'given' which puts humankind in a radically new perspective. And this given negates, radically again, the primary feature of politics and science, which is control. Control is the other side of the coin of "responsible decision." It is the demon which must continually be exorcised to prevent the utopias from becoming the dystopias. And apocalyptic literature, both intertestamental, biblical, and current secular apocalyptic (science fiction) is the means with which to perform the exorcism.

The final line to be drawn, from the racial down to the technocratic is the most difficult. This is so because it participates to some degree in both the monarchic-political and in the universalist-philosophical. This was the case with the racial in biblical history: it preserved its political base while seeking new forms of being. The result was theocracy, the kingdom of God in this world, established by the coming in glory of God himself or his messiah. There is a future rising out of the present, but at the same time (meeting it halfway, as it were) comes the future breaking into the present. So also in this particular branch of science fiction we encounter a form which participates in both the political and the philosophical, although being a form all its own. If it presents a utopia, it presents a scientific and technological utopia, based on a new advance in the field. If it speculates about the nature and destiny of humankind, it does so in scientific and technological categories, grounded solidly in the hard, physical sciences. And it blends both of these together into a *belief* in the future, a future which will see the perfection of humankind in both the political and scientific forms; namely, a technocracy. In a technocracy the two interpenetrate; good politics will be good technology, and good technology will be good politics. The horizon is technocratic.

The crisis addressed is a crisis of belief—again, one which incorporates both a crisis of will and a crisis of vision, without being reduced to either alone. If, among the triumvirate of science fiction writers from its "golden age," Heinlein represents the political branch, and Clarke the philosophical, then Asimov represents the technocratic, in terms spelled out above. Heinlein plays with new political forms, both societal and familial, in *Stranger in a Strange Land*, and *The Moon is a Harsh Mistress*, and in his *Future History* collection. In the end he always comes down to the question of how we are to live together, whether in large or small groups. Clarke always speculates on the much larger issues, as noted above. Asimov, on the other hand, in the *Foundation* trilogy and in *I, Robot*, to cite but two examples, always does some of each, but always again only insofar as he is grounded solidly in the hard, physical sciences. We have noted above the "breakthrough" of psychohistory (based on the mathematization of psychology) in *Foundation*, and the philosophical musings of the robots in *I, Robot*. These are but two examples which illustrate the pull from both sides. But in the end, the care and planning of and for the future depends not on will, not on vision, but on a faith in and a commitment to science and technology. This faith and commitment, moreover, is "racial"—in the sense that it belongs to the entire race of intelligent beings, not to some small elite, whether it be political, scientific, or philosophical. Anyone can believe—even the robots!

The technocratic horizon represents the mainstream of science fiction, comprising the bulk of its stories and novels. In this it also reflects the movement in the Bible, where both the monarchic and the philosophical branches are pushed off to the edges. Both are necessary in the process of memory and hope, but neither alone is able to carry faithfully the promise of God. In the Bible it is the faith, the belief in God working in and through human history (i.e., through the decisions made by believing subjects) which is the core. In science fiction it is the belief in science and technology, engaged in by responsible human beings, which will ultimately bring about a better future.

5) All this is seen more clearly in the next series of categories listed in the chart: the ideas about history and salvation, the problem of death and its correlative, immortality, and the final goal of history and creation. Most of this is self-explanatory and is based in the categories and distinctions made by Buber and others between prophecy and apocalyptic. The new element here, perhaps, is the way in which the monarchic-political, the racial-technocratic, and the universalist-philosophical respond to the question of immortality. Using again the triumvirate of Heinlein, Asimov and Clarke, it is interesting to note Heinlein's obsession with personal, physical immortality (whether through brain transplant, cloning, or selective breeding of longevity lines to achieve virtual immortality); Asimov's continued emphasis on the immortality of the human race of intelligent beings in their present forms (people are always people; they live and die, but the race goes on); and Clarke's mystical revelations of transformations into eternal life of mind and spirit, wherein all will be absorbed into the Overmind or some other super-intelligence.

Are these different conceptions of death and immortality in any way necessary? Is there any causal connection between the preceding categorizations and this final category? I think so. Although it is commonplace and quite appropriate to speak of the will of the people, the common, general or popular will; still, will is an act which is most often associated specifically and irrevocably with a single, individual, specified, concrete human being. Even when it is applied to the general public, it is always to a single, individual, specified concrete public. Will does not exist even imaginatively outside the concrete perpetrator of will. For will to survive (and survival is the confirmation of being, its blessing and reward), the individual, specified, concrete human being must survive as is. Personal, physical immortality seems to be the logical and psychological adjunct to the literature which focuses on will.

This is not the case with belief, however. Here the focal point is precisely the collective, the community. Belief exists to be handed on, to be shared. An individual belief, privately held, dies with the person who holds that belief; but a belief which is shared by a community lives on, no matter that the individual dies. And the opposite is also true: the community must be immortal if the belief is to survive. Racial immortality, then, is a logical and psychological adjunct to a literature which focuses on belief. Even if, in the post-catastrophe stories of science fiction, it is only a small group of people who survive, what always survives along with them is their belief (usually in a small but critical collection of the books necessary to preserve the beneficent technology). Both the knowledge and the people necessary to live out that knowledge survive. Either alone is not enough. The people must survive in some form of community, even if the community is only linked to the present community by the most tenuous of means: radio contact, descended over a long journey through space, or the survivors of the final war.

In the final branch of science fiction, no such continuity exists. Immortality is always a transformation into some higher and beyond the present sphere of existence. That is, immortality is achieved by breaking the connection with the present world, losing the physical, material restraints, and being absorbed into the larger whole, usually super-mind or super-intelligence. Immortality is achieved by leaving behind what is individual, what is human, and what is physical and material. Only the mind and/or the spirit passes on to immortality. Ideas, that is, have a life of their own. Immortality, in this branch, reflects the universalist themes; there are no national, political or even racial boundaries. Nor is immortality achieved by any ordinary, logical, systematic progression; nor, least of all, does it rise out of the action of belief of some one individual or group. Nor, finally, does it even depend on the survival of any human beings: the ideas and the super-mind are subsistent in themselves. The best that mankind can do is share in that already existing immortality—and this can only be done through a spiritual transformation, effected from outside and worked on minds and spirits who have taken the necessary steps, i.e., rendered themselves passive to the transformation. This immortality, then, is a confirmation of the life style of the apocalyptic branch of science fiction, in much the same manner that each particular type of immortality confirms the understanding and life style implicit in its own main thrust.

6) I will conclude with some reflections on the literary qualities of the three branches of science fiction, using as my main examples again the writings of Heinlein, Asimov and Clarke. This is literary critical more in the manner of structure than in the matter of style; that is, it touches on the history of ideas, and their theology also, their generation, and the forms they assume in popular literature.

To begin, I have listed realism, romance and myth as the three literary forms (or structures, if you will), corresponding to the three branches of science fiction. Of course there is much overlapping; but I trust the main outline will be somewhat evident. Realism is the form which a political literature takes when confronted with the task of telling a story about the future of humankind. Its tendency is to become episodic, sequential and chronological. This happened and then this happened and finally this. The sequential connections are quite detailed and rather easy to follow. There is rarely any difficulty in summarizing the plot of this kind of story. Action follows upon action. That is, it is much harder to see the causal connections between the sequence of events. This becomes apparent when one tries to retell the story, summarize the plot, in another way. It is hard to do. In the end it is evident that there are few if any ideas or understandings behind the sequence of events. The story is rarely about an idea which explains the actions of the characters; it is simply and almost entirely about the actions themselves.

Most of the later writings of Robert Heinlein fall into his category. They are almost entirely episodic and sequential. There is always a lot going on; but eventually one reaches the point of asking: Why does all this keep going on? What's the meaning, anyway. *Time Enough for Love* continues upon *Stranger in a Strange Land,* the book in which Heinlein switched style in midstream, to the type of writing which reaches fruition in his latest book, *The Number of the Beast.* There is *no* point to this book, although (or perhaps, because) it is a simple matter to summarize exactly and succinctly what happens. And what happens is this—to attempt some formulation of the idea behind the book, the understanding of life, world, history, and future—people decide to do things! When people take their destiny into their own hands, then things will work out; or, at the very least, it will be terribly exciting and fulfilling while it lasts. This is the further point behind the book; and in this it fits in with many other features of this branch of science fiction: it emphasizes will and responsibility for the future, using from the past only the examples of strong-minded persons as models for present and future decisions, and creates a future totally dependent upon its own actions. The next episode will not happen until and unless the character decides it will happen.

Any continuity in this type of literature can only be understood in terms of the decisions made by the characters; and they are not in any way determined in those decisions except to know that it depends on them. Whatever happens depends on them. They head into the future more or less blind to any larger picture. It is exciting and interesting; but it is not going anywhere in particular because there is nowhere in particular to go. It simply continues until it stops. There is no real "end," in the sense of a goal. At the most, the "end" is to stay alive so that history can continue; because once the individual stops, that's it, there is no more. Motivation, in this literature, is reduced to the need to survive. Certainly this is a worthwhile and adequate motive in many cases; but hardly sufficient to explain the past in its entirety, or inspire the future in its fullness. Yet when all else fails— and this is the bottom line, explaining perhaps the enduring appeal of this type of literature—survival is a worthwhile motive. Yet a further question remains, a question the instinct for survival cannot itself explain, why survive? For this we must move on to the next branch of science fiction, the racial-technocratic and its literary form, the romance.

Romance is the story told by the racial-technocratic branch of science fiction when it confronts the question of motivation and the deeper understandings of human actions. In many of its features it is similar to realism, as discussed above. But only on the surface. It, too, sometimes tends to become episodic, sequential and merely chronological. But the wider picture is always there; the frame is always evident. One always knows who is telling the story, to whom, and why it is being told. There is one central thread running through the whole tale, a story-line which can be summarized quite easily in the form of an idea or a message: "the moral of the story is . . . ." The story itself exists to carry the message; its purpose is to get the point across. It is, as many critics have pointed out, a didactic literature. All literature is didactic to some degree or other, but romance (especially science fiction romance) is consciously and blatantly didactic.

What it teaches, however, is contained not only in the content of the story; it is also carried in the form. It seeks to make evident the causal connections, not only the sequential ones. Its message is that there can be an order and a plan to what happens in the future, but such order and plan depends on what is decided now. And what is decided now depends on more than a simple, blind act of will; it depends on an order and plan derived from a faith, a belief. No one can say for sure what the future will be; we have no certain knowledge in hard, physical categories. It is faith alone which makes known to us both the order and the means to arrive at that order. This faith, moreover, is not something private and interior; it exists within the larger reality, shared by a community of believers. The believer tells the story to other believers for the sake of the belief, its promulgation and its strengthening. Faith is never merely for entertainment or diversion; it is always deadly serious. It does make a difference. It explains things, it confirms, it justifies, not the individual, but the individual within the larger order of reality—that is, where the person fits into both space and time. It tells not only about the future, but also about how that future is to be achieved. Its faith makes sense out of what has happened in the past, what is happening now, and what will be happening in the future.

This faith is nothing other than the belief in science and technology, as explored above in Chapter Two. It has less to do with technology than with technique, however, to use the distinction insisted on by Ellul. To use Asimov's thought: gadget science fiction gives way to social science fiction. Asimov is the prime example here of the science fiction romance. His theory of science fiction comes from reflection on his practice. He is always more concerned with the message than with the gadget. The positronic brain has long since been superseded, in fact as well as in fiction. But the three laws of robotics live on, and perhaps always will. They are a faith statement about the order which should exist in the relationships between intelligent beings. They cannot be proved or disproved, verified or falsified. They are either accepted or rejected as is. It is the technique rather than the technology which is manifested in Asimov's stories. All the robot stories are exercises in technique. The fact that the form closely follows the mystery/crime genre only makes the faith in the technique stand out that more clearly. Technologies may change (as, indeed, they have, both in science fiction and in crime solving: Holmes gave way to Poirot, who himself gives way); but the technique always remains the same: the systematic and rigorous and scientific examination of facts until the larger picture emerges. No detail is irrelevant in the story; all will eventually and inevitably come together in the end.

This is perhaps the most important thing to be said about the romance: it does have an end, in the sense of a goal. It is literature written from the end. Without that end, it would make no sense. It is the end which unifies and explains. The point, then, of the romance is the end and the ending. And this is precisely the message carried by the form itself: that there is an end, and that the end will make sense of everything that has gone before. Survival is important, therefore, only in the sense of surviving to keep the faith alive, to share it and pass it on. Even if it is necesary to go into eclipse and remain hidden for centuries on end (as in *Foundation*), still it must be kept alive. Likewise, the real breakthrough to history occurs when there is a faith to pass on (a faith which makes some sense of what is happening). This is what happens in Asimov's "Nightfall," wherein each succeeding age painfully suffers collapse until the scientists discover that the darkness of night (nightfall) is a regularly occurring event (albeit, on a planet with multiple suns, it happens only rarely) which can be understood and predicted according to scientific laws. When such a faith emerges, then the story can proceed along a linear path, stretching off into the future, leaving behind the cyclical view of history. Without it all is cycle and chaos.

It is interesting, finally, that a large part of the racial-technocratic branch of science fiction concerns itself with demythologization, the attempt to explain seemingly supernatural events in natural terms, hard, physical, cause/effect categories. "Nightfall" consciously does this; but all of its stories and most others of this type engage in the same activity. The horizon is larger than the monarchic-political, but is still well within human enterprise and knowledge. Someday we will know and do all that is possible to know and do.

It is here, however, that we pass over into the universalist-philosophical branch of science fiction, and its predominant literary form, myth. Although, as some have argued, there is little to distinguish myth and romance structurally (see especially Northrop Frye, *The Secular Scripture*); and although the "history of religions" definition of myth as story peopled with divine beings has fallen into general disfavor, still there are differences between romance and myth, and those differences have much to do with the "divine beings." It is here perhaps where science fiction presents us with the clearest example of what myth is and how it functions in a society. Science fiction certainly has its divine beings; and sometimes even a divine being closely resembling God. That is not the point, however. Such parallels ultimately lead down the wrong path.

The point about divine beings is that they symbolize the limits of human enterprise and knowledge—limits which can never be breached, no matter what the human effort through natural intelligence or with the aid of machines, or finally, and perhaps most significantly, no matter what the human effort expended to survive until the end is reached. The "end" of the romance, its goal and conclusion, is a limit which can and must be achieved in the story (and history) of humankind. There may be no other limits, as all good technocrats say, to what the human race can do; but there is a limit, in the sense of an end to the story and the history of humankind.

The universalist-philosophical branch of science fiction, that is, secular apocalyptic, confronts this problem head on. If there are limits ultimately, it argues, then there are limits all along the line. If in the whole sweep of human history, from the first stirrings of consciousness and intelligence to the final magnificent achievement of having understood the inner secrets of life and the universe, there is never the possibility of surpassing what it means to be human, then what is the point? Why speak of the unlimited, when we are limited radically here and now—by our method and by our object? To the universalist-philosophical branch, all that the racial-technocratic branch has done is to expand the cycle of history so enormously that from our present station the line along which we are travelling appears to be straight—when in reality it is curving ever so slowly to complete ultimately the loop. The end, indeed, makes sense of all that has gone before; but in this case it means only that all along the line we face limits. Or, as the apocalyptic branch would put it, we have limited ourselves all along the line by the very fact that we have limited ourselves by the end. This is where and how myth returns.

The central, operative theme of apocalyptic is the myth of the end which is *not* an end, but a passage into a new time which has no end! It is truly a new age, not just another age which unfolds temporally as does this present age. For apocalyptic there has to be another time, for this time is limited. This is the key to the other world which exists now, the other world which knows no limits. For only that which has no limits can truly be a limit for that which is limited. This, then, is the true limit of human enterprise and intelligence, the unlimited—but not the unlimited of its own divising.

Thus, in this world now we encounter those "divine beings" who cannot be explained away by natural means or by an appeal to newly discovered natural laws. Truly we are not alone. Just as once you admit the existence of an end which is not the end, thereby necessarily admitting all along the line the existence of beings which are more than human; so also, once you admit the existence of beings which are divine, then you also must admit the existence of an end which is really not the end. Once, that is, you admit the existence of God, then there cannot be a *human* end to history. This is the great discovery of apocalyptic thought in biblical times. It has been "discovered" repeatedly down through human history, to the current discovery again in both theology and science fiction. Along with this discovery there comes a new appreciation of immortality: to be immortal means to participate somehow in that which is immortal, the unlimited. All the above themes and understandings are illustrated clearly in Clarke's *Childhood's End*. But the most striking feature of that book is the temporal narrative structure. It reflects a radically altered understanding of time. There is here no ordinary flow of events in tight narrative sequence. Episode does not follow episode, as in Heinlein. Not only to the main characters shift throughout the book, so also does the focus of time shift. It is as though there is another time in which the book is set. And that is the point!

Notes

Introduction
[1]Peter Berger, *The Sacred Canopy* (Garden City: Doubleday, 1967), p. 28.

Chapter One
[1]The best short treatment of apocalyptic thought and literature is D.S. Russell's *Apocalyptic: Ancient and Modern* (Philadelphia: Fortress, 1977). In addition to the studies on apocalyptic by Hanson, Rowley, Schmithals and Collins, quoted below in the notes, I have also relied on Otto Ploger, *Theocracy and Eschatology* (Richmond: John Knox, 1968), a longer study by D.S. Russell, *The Method and Message of Jewish Apocalyptic* (London: SCM Press, 1969); Klaus Koch, *The Rediscovery of Apocalyptic* (Naperville: Allenson, 1970); and my own previous study, *Apocalypse and Science Fiction* (Chico: Scholars Press, 1982).

[2]"The Politics of Immortality: A Conversation with Robert Jay Lifton and T. George Harris," *Psychology Today* 4:6 (Nov., 1970), p. 40.

[3]See Norman Cohn, *The Pursuit of the Millennium* (New York: Oxford, 1970), p. 34.

[4]Philip Jose Farmer, *Doc Savage: His Apocalyptic Life* (New York: Bantam, 1975).

[5]Bob Dylan, "I Shall be Free," from the album, *The Freewheelin' Bob Dylan* (Columbia Records, CS 8786).

[6]Bob Dylan, "Talkin' World War III Blues," the same album.

[7]Romano Guardini, *The Lord* (Chicago: Regnery, 1954), p. 502.

[8]Bob Dylan: quoted by Nat Hentoff on the jacket cover notes for the album *The Free Wheelin' Bob Dylan*.

[9]Bob Dylan, "It's All Over Now, Baby Blue," from the album *Bringing It All Back Home* (Columbia Records, CS 9128).

[10]See *Apocalypse and Science Fiction* (Note 1), especially pp. 211-219.

[11]Jorma Kaukonen, "Star Track," from the Jefferson Airplane album *Crown of Creation* (RCA, AYL-1-3797).

[12]Jorma Kaukonen, "Ice Cream Phoenix," the same album.

[13]Paul Kantner, "Crown of Creation," the same album.

[14]John Wyndham, *Re-Birth* (New York: Ballantine, 1955), pp. 168, 181.

[15]Paul Kantner, Martin Balin, "The House at Pooneil Corners," from the *Crown of Creation* album.

[16]Paul Kantner, Grace Slick, Marty Balin, "Hijack," from the Jefferson Starship Album *Blows Against the Empire* (RCA, AYL 1-3868).

[17]Paul Kantner, Grace Slick, Marty Balin, "Starship," the same album.

Chapter Two

[1]Jacques Ellul, *The Technological Society* (New York: Vintage, 1964), p. 97.

[2]Ibid., p. 22.

[3]Ibid., p. 7.

[4]Langdon Gilkey, from an address to a gathering of Nobel laureates at Gustavus Adolphus College in St. Peter, Minnesota, 1975, unpublished.

[5]Brian W. Aldiss, *Billion Year Spree* (New York: Schocken, 1974), p. 232.

[6]Isaac Asimov, *Second Foundation* (New York: Avon, 1964), p. 86 (Chapter 8).

[7]Ellul, *The Technological Society*, p. 97.

[8]Ibid., p. 141.

[9]John W. Campbell, Jr., "The Place of Science Fiction in the Modern World," in Reginald Bretnor, ed., *Modern Science Fiction* (New York: Coward-McCann, 1953), p. 11.

[10]Frederik Pohl and C.M. Kornbluth, *The Space Merchants* (New York: Ballantine, 1953), p. 16.

[11]Ellul, *The Technological Society*, p. 89.

[12]See Theodor H. Gaster, *Thespis* (Garden City: Anchor Doubleday, 1961), p. 41.

[13]Marshall McLuhan, *Understanding Media* (New York: Signet, 1966), p. 56.

[14]See Arthur C. Clarke, *Profiles of the Future* (New York: Bantam, 1964), especially p. 197-211.

[15]Buckminster Fuller, *Utopia or Oblivion* (New York: Bantam, 1969), p. 224.

[16]Ellul, *The Technological Society*, p. 135.

[17]Arthur C. Clarke, *Childhood's End* (New York: Ballantine, 1953), p. 205.

[18]McLuhan, *Understanding Media*, p. 55.

[19]Reprinted everywhere. Most readily available in Isaac Asimov, *I, Robot* (Greenwich: Fawcett Crest, 1970), p. 6.

[20]Ibid., p. 51-52.

[21]Ibid., p. 169.

[22]Ibid., p. 192.

[23]David Ketterer, *New Worlds for Old* (Garden City: Doubleday Anchor, 1974), p. 76.

Chapter Three

[1]Gary K. Wolfe, "The Known and the Unknown: Structure and Image in Science Fiction," in Thomas D. Clareson, ed., *Many Futures, Many Worlds* (Kent: Kent State University Press, 1977), p. 113.

[2]This passage is taken, with apologies, from Giles Gunn, "Threading the Eye of the Needle: The Place of the Literary Critic in Religious Studies," *JAAR* XLIII (June, 1975), p. 182.

[3]Ibid., p. 182.

[4]Ibid., p. 183.

[5]See Norman Cohn, *The Pursuit of the Millennium*, pp. 108-113, for a discusison of Joachim of Fiore.

[6]Edmund Bacon, "The City Image," in Elizabeth Green, Jeanne R. Lowe and Kenneth Walker, eds., *Man and the Modern City* (Pittsburgh, 1963), p. 25.

[7]Jacques Ellul, *The Meaning of the City* (Grand Rapids: Eerdmans, 1970), p. 162.

[8]B.F. Skinner, *Walden Two* (New York: Macmillan, 1962), p. 115.

[9]Ibid., pp. 238-39.

[10]Ibid., p. 235.

[11]Lewis Mumford, *The City in History* (New York: Harcourt, Brace and World, 1961), p. 526.

[12]Sam Bass Warner, *The Urban Wilderness* (New York: Harper & Row),1972, p. 4.

[13]Grady Clay, *Close-Up: How to Read the American City* (New York: Praeger, 1973), p. 14.

[14]Auchincloss' statement is quoted in Alvin Toffler, *Future Shock* (New York: Bantam, 1971), p. 55.

[15]Anselm Strauss, *Images of the American City* (New York: Free Press, 1961), p. 25.

[16]Sir John Summerson, "Urban Forms," in Oscar Handlin and John Burchard, eds., *The Historian and the City* (Cambridge: MIT Press, 1963), p. 167. Summerson is commenting on Patrick Geddes' contribution to the historical study of the city.

[17]E.A. Speiser, *Genesis: The Anchor Bible* (Garden City: Doubleday, 1964), p. 36.

[18]See Henri Gougard, *Demons et Merveilles de la Science Fiction* (Paris: Julliard, 1974), pp. 83-99.

[19]Thomas Pynchon, *The Crying of Lot 49* (New York: Bantam, 1967), p. 12.

[20]In Rogert Elwood, ed., *Future City* (New York: Pocket Books, 1974), p. 240.

[21]James Blish, *A Case of Conscience* (London: Arrow Books, 1972), pp. 104-105.

[22]See the discussion of the "Second Death" in Jonathan Schell, *The Fate of the Earth* (London: Picador, 1982), pp. 97-178.

[23]Guardini, *The Lord*, p. 522.

[24]Clarke, *Childhood's End*, pp. 74-75.

[25]Philip K. Dick, *The Man in the High Castle* (New York: Berkley, 1962), p. 249.

[26]Ibid., p. 251.

[27]Philip K. Dick, *The Penultimate Truth* (New York: Belmont, 1964), pp. 60-61.

[28]See Rudolph Bultmann, "New Testament Mythology," in Hans Warner Bertsch, ed., *Kergyma and Myth: A Theological Debate* (New York: Harper Torchbooks, 1961), pp. 1-44.

Chapter Four

[1]Gernsback's editorial is reprinted in various places. The most accessible, perhaps, is in James Gunn, *Alternate Worlds* (Englewood Cliffs: Prentice Hall, 1975), pp. 120-121.

[2]J.O.Bailey, *Pilgrims Through Time and Space* (Westport: Greenwood, 1972, reissue), p. 10.

[3]Willis E. McNelley, ed., *Science Fiction: The Academic Awakening* (CEA Chapbook, 1974), passim.

[4]John W. Campbell, Jr., "The Place of Science Fiction ..." p. 17.

[5]Oscar Schaftel, "The Social Content of Science Fiction," *Science and Society* 17 (Spring, 1953), p. 115. For further discussion of science fiction as 'future planning,' see Thomas Scortia, "Science Fiction as the Imaginary Experiment," in Reginal Bretnor, ed., *Science Fiction: Today and Tomorrow* (Baltimore: Penguin,1974), pp. 135-49; and Steven Kagle, "Science Fiction as Simulation Game," in Clareson, ed., *Many Futures, Many Worlds*, pp. 224-36. The phrase 'admonitory utopia' is from Kingsley Amis, *New Maps of Hell* (New York: Harcourt, Brace, 1960).

[6]Robert Kellog and Robert Scholes, *The Nature of Narrative* (New York: Oxford, 1966), p. 82.

[7]Mark R. Hillegas, "Science Fiction as a Cultural Phenomenon," in Thomas D. Clareson, ed., *SF: The Other Side of Realism* (Bowling Green: Popular Press, 1971), p. 276.

[8]Ketterer, *New Worlds for Old*, p. 123.

[9]Ibid., pp. 13-17.

[10]Robert Canary, "Science Fiction as Fictive History," in Clareson, ed., *Many Futures, Many Worlds*, p. 178.

[11]Ibid., p. 170.

[12]Robert Scholes, *Structural Fabulation* (Notre Dame: Univ. of Notre Dame Press, 1975), p. 75. Author's emphasis.

[13]Ben Bova, *Millennium* (New York: Ballantine, 1977), p. 19.

[14]Ibid., p. 224.

[15]Piers Anthony, *Battle Circle* (New York: Avon, 1978), p. 135.

[16]Ibid., p. 511.

[17]Buber's schema, like Gernsback's editorial, is reprinted in various places. The most currently accessible is in Paul D. Hanson, *The Dawn of Apocalyptic* (Philadelphia: Fortress, 1975), p. 5. The schematization is not Buber's, however, as Hanson makes clear in his note: Martin Buber, *Kampf um Israel; Reden und Schriften* (Berlin: Schocken Verlag, 1933), pp. 59ff.

[18]See Ernest Kasemann, *New Testament Questions of Today* (Philadelphia: Fortress, 1969), pp. 82-107.

[19]Frank Kermode, *The Sense of an Ending* (New York: Oxford, 1967), p. 6.

[20]Hanson, *The Dawn of Apocalyptic*, p. 11.

[21]Kreuziger, *Apocalypse and Science Fiction*, pp. 98-135.

[22]Ursula LeGuin, *The Dispossessed* (New York: Avon,1974), p. 225.

[23]Ernest Callenback, *Ecotopia* (New York: Bantam, 1977), pp. 212-13.

[24]Walker Percy, *Love in the Ruins* (New York: Avon, 1978), p. 60.

[25]Doris Lessing, *The Four-Gated City* (New York: Bantam, 1970), pp.

604-05.
[26]Percy, *Love in the Ruins*, p. 196.
[27]Lessing, *The Four-Gated City*, pp. 524-25.
[28]LeGuin, *The Dispossessed*, p. 177.
[29]Ibid., p. 228.
[30]Percy, *Love in the Ruins*, p. 360.
[31]Lessing, *The Four-Gated City*, p. 453.
[32]LeGuin, *The Dispossessed*, p. 267.
[33]Percy, *Love in the Ruins*, pp. 44-45.
[34]Ibid., p. 363.
[35]Lessing, *The Four-Gated City*, p. 590.

Chapter Five

[1]Martin Buber, *Pointing the Way* (New York: Harper and Row, 1957), p. 203.
[2]Nathan Scott, Jr., " 'New Heav'ns, New Earth,'—The Landscape of Contemporary Apocalypse," *Journal of Religion*, 53, p. 5.
[3]Ibid., p. 9.
[4]Ibid., p. 12.
[5]Ibid., pp. 18-30.
[6]Ibid., p. 35.
[7]Walter Schmithals, *The Apocalyptic Movement: Introduction and Interpretation* (Nashville: Abingdon, 1975), p. 40.
[8]Ibid., pp. 78-80.
[9]Ibid., p. 146.
[10]J. Norman King, "Theology, Science Fiction and Man's Future Orientation," in Clareson, ed., *Many Futures, Many Worlds*, pp. 241-42.
[11]Ibid., p. 244.
[12]Ibid., pp. 244-45.
[13]Walter Hirsch, "The Image of the Scientist in Science Fiction: A Content Analysis," *American Journal of Sociology*, 63, p. 511.
[14]Andrew Greeley, "When Religion Cast Off Wonder, Hollywood Seized It," *The New York Times* (Nov. 27, 1977).
[15]King, "Theology, Science Fiction . . . ," p. 245.
[16]See J.B. Metz, "For a Renewed Church before a New Council: A Concept in Four Theses," in David Tracy, ed., *Toward Vatican III: The Work That Needs to Be Done* (New York: Seabury, 1978), pp. 143-45.
[17]Teilhard de Chardin, *The Future of Man* (New York: Harper, 1964), p. 130.
[18]Ibid., p. 141.
[19]Ibid., p. 143.
[20]Langdon Gilkey, *Reaping the Whirlwind* (New York: Seabury, 1977), p. 144.
[21]Ibid., p. 153.
[22]Ibid., p. 251.
[23]Ibid., p. 231.
[24]Ibid., p. 234.

[25] J. Gunn, *Alternate Worlds*, p. 225.

[26] These themes of secular apocalyptic are treated in detail in my *Apocalypse and Science Fiction*, pp. 12-50.

[27] J.J. Collins, "Apocalyptic Eschatology as the Transcendence of Death," *CBQ* 36, pp. 21-43.

[28] The 'Enoch' and 'Ezra' passages are from R. Charles, *The Apocrypha and Pseudoepigripha of the Old Testament* II (Oxford, 1913).

Chapter Six

[1] H.H. Rowley, *The Relevance of Apocalyptic* (London: Lutterworth, 1944).

[2] Basically the pre-millennialists hold that a 'thousand year reign' by the just will precede the second coming of Christ; the millennialists, that the second coming will inaugurate the thousand year reign. See E.R. Sandeen, *The Roots of Fundamentalism* (Chicago: Univ. of Chicago Press, 1970).

[3] See Huston Smith, *Forgotten Truth: The Primordial Tradition* (New York: Harper, 1976). The reader will find supporting arguments in E.F. Schumacher, *A Guide for the Perplexed* (New York: Harper & Row, 1977); and in a book which has only recently come to my attention, Walker Percy, *Lost in the Cosmos: The Last Self-Help Book* (New York: Farrar, Straus & Giroux, 1983).